☆ **Contents** ☆

AMERICAN
WAR LIBRARY
★ ★ ★ ★

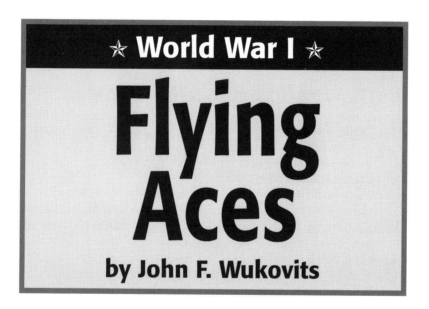

★ World War I ★

Flying Aces

by John F. Wukovits

Lucent Books, 10911 Technology Place, San Diego, CA 92127

Titles in The American War Library series include:

World War II
Hitler and the Nazis
Kamikazes
Leaders and Generals
Life as a POW
Life of an American Soldier in
 Europe
Strategic Battles in Europe
Strategic Battles in the Pacific
The War at Home
Weapons of War

The Civil War
Leaders of the North and South
Life Among the Soldiers and
 Cavalry
Lincoln and the Abolition of
 Slavery
Strategic Battles
Weapons of War

Library of Congress Cataloging-in-Publication Data

Wukovits, John F., 1944–
  Flying aces / by John F. Wukovits.
    p. cm. — (American war library. World War I)
Includes bibliographical references and index.
Summary: Recounts the lives and aerial achievements of some of
the most famous flying aces in World War I, including Manfred von
Richthofen, Eddie Rickenbacker, Edward "Mick" Mannock, Albert
Ball, Jr., Rene Fonck, and Georges Guynemer.
  ISBN 1-56006-810-8 (hardback)
  1. World War, 1914–1918—Aerial operation—Juvenile
literature. 2. Fighter pilots—Biography—Juvenile literature.
3. World War, 1914–1918—Biography—Juvenile literature.
[1. Fighter pilots. 2. World War, 1914–1918—Aerial operations.
3. World War, 1914–1918—Biography.] I. Title. II. Series.
  D600 .W85 2002
  940.4'4'0922—dc21

2001004402

A Nation Forged by War

The United States, like many nations, was forged and defined by war. Despite Benjamin Franklin's opinion that "There never was a good war or a bad peace," the United States owes its very existence to the War of Independence, one to which Franklin wholeheartedly subscribed. The country forged by war in 1776 was tempered and made stronger by the Civil War in the 1860s.

The Texas Revolution, the Mexican-American War, and the Spanish-American War expanded the country's borders and gave it overseas possessions. These wars made the United States a world power, but this status came with a price, as the nation became a key but reluctant player in both World War I and World War II.

Each successive war further defined the country's role on the world stage. Following World War II, U.S. foreign policy redefined itself to focus on the role of defender, not only of the freedom of its own citizens, but also of the freedom of people everywhere. During the cold war that followed World War II until the collapse of the Soviet Union, defending the world meant fighting communism. This goal, manifested in the Korean and Vietnam conflicts, proved elusive, and soured the American public on its achievability. As the United States emerged as the world's sole superpower, American foreign policy has been guided less by national interest and more on protecting international human rights. But as involvement in Somalia and Kosovo prove, this goal has been equally elusive.

As a result, the country's view of itself changed. Bolstered by victories in World Wars I and II, Americans first relished the role of protector. But, as war followed war in a seemingly endless procession, Americans began to doubt their leaders, their motives, and themselves. The Vietnam War especially caused people to question the validity of sending its young people to die in places where they were not particularly wanted and for people who did not seem especially grateful.

While the most obvious changes brought about by America's wars have been geopolitical in nature, many other aspects of society have been touched. War often does not bring about change directly, but acts instead like the catalyst in a chemical reaction, accelerating changes already in progress.

Some of these changes have been societal. The role of women in the United States had been slowly changing, but World War II put thousands into the workforce and into uniform. They might have gone back to being housewives after the war, but equality, once experienced, would not be forgotten.

Likewise, wars have accelerated technological change. The necessity for faster airplanes and a more destructive bomb led to the development of jet planes and nuclear energy. Artificial fibers developed for parachutes in the 1940s were used in the clothing of the 1950s.

Lucent Books' American War Library covers key wars in the development of the nation. Each war is covered in several volumes, to allow for more detail, context, and to provide volumes on often neglected subjects, such as the kamikazes of World War II, or weapons used in the Civil War. As with all Lucent Books, notes, annotated bibliographies, and appendixes such as glossaries give students a launching point for further research. In addition, sidebars and archival photographs enhance the text. Together, each volume in The American War Library will aid students in understanding how America's wars have shaped and changed its politics, economics, and society.

"It Was Like a Sport"

Aerial combat in World War I has long been romanticized. History has often depicted the fliers as larger-than-life heroes who gallantly stepped to their machines, lifted to the heavens, and dashed into battle with a carefree attitude that scorned death and disdained danger. One-on-one combat between opposing pilots stirred the soul and conjured images of the battle days of yore, when medieval knights donned suits of armor and fought on horseback.

Only in the skies, though, is individual fighting viewed as clean and noble. Hand-to-hand fighting by infantry on the ground, where men grab, choke, gouge, shoot, and bayonet at close range, produces terror and fright, but deadly battle in the skies above yields honor and dignity. World War I aviators offered numerous examples of honorable demeanor, yet they also provided instances of stunning brutality. Some pilots headed into the air with remarkable joy while others lifted off assuming that they would die before returning.

Although aerial combat is often glamorized, numerous WWI flight missions ended in disaster.

7

War Takes to the Skies

Romantic notions of World War I combat in the air exist in part because fighting had always been confined to the ground or the seas. Never before in history had men mounted weapons to aircraft and engaged their enemy at high speed. They provided a visual spectacle to their infantry cohorts below, who watched in fascination as fabric-covered machines raced toward one another in death-defying duels.

Airpower played a major military role right from the beginning of World War I. Thirty-seven aircraft accompanied the first British troops to cross the English Channel and head into battle against the Germans in August 1914, shortly after the war's outbreak. The slow, lumbering aircraft were not designed for battle—the unarmed craft's main purpose was for observing enemy positions and movement. In those heady first weeks of war, French and British aviators frequently flew directly by their German counterparts without a thought of fighting—instead they gaily waved to each other.

That quickly changed when airmen first took weapons along and began shooting at their opponents. In an effort to provide protection for the observation plane and its two airmen—a pilot and an observer—single-seaters bearing machine guns or rifles began to accompany the observation air-

craft. In February 1915, French pilot Roland Garros mounted a gun that fired bullets through his propeller. This handed Garros an advantage, but since the firing was not synchronized with the propeller's rotation, he never knew when a bullet might smack into his own propeller blade and send him

French pilot Roland Garros was the first to earn the name "ace" for his bravery in aerial combat.

careening to the ground. Garros disregarded the danger and shot down five aircraft in less than three weeks, thereby becoming warfare's first "ace," a name used by the French to describe an outstanding performer in any field. The appellation would be quickly adopted by pilots of all nations.

In July 1915, Capt. Lanoe Hawker of the British Royal Flying Corps mounted a rifle on the right side of his aircraft in such a position that he could fly and shoot at the same time. The bullets sped off to the side of the propeller rather than passing directly through, but it meant that he had to approach his quarry from the side rather than head-on. Hawker gained notoriety that same month by downing two German planes in one day and earning his nation's highest military honor, the Victoria Cross.

Aviators commanded increasing notice in the summer of 1916, when titanic aerial battles filled the skies above France, particularly over Verdun and the Somme River. Both sides realized by then that one had to control the air to gain the advantage on the ground. Officers made the dual assertion that you could not win land battles without controlling the skies and you could not lose if you commanded the heavens.

The final piece in aerial combat appeared in April 1917 when the United States entered the war. The nation could not offer much at first, since the sorry plight of the country's Aviation Section—only 130 officers and 250 aircraft—precluded a signifi-

Enemies, Friends

Opposing airmen held each other in great regard. They faced common dangers, engaged in similar missions, and experienced situations that men in other branches of the military did not. This sometimes led to touching episodes.

One such case occurred between the French aviator Jacques Herbelin and the German airman Joachim Leopold. The two engaged in battle over France, where Herbelin shot down Leopold. The German survived his injuries, and the two men started a friendship that lasted well beyond the war. In 1942, after Adolf Hitler's armies had conquered much of France, Leopold returned to Paris as part of the Nazi government of the capital. One day he learned that the German secret police, the Gestapo, intended to arrest his old friend from World War I. Leopold risked death by sending a message warning Herbelin to flee. The French aviator departed before the German authorities arrived.

cant contribution. But once American pilots collected in large numbers, they tipped the advantage to the Allied side.

"Ah, the Girls, Old Man"

World War I flying aces have fashioned a legend of their own, rarely equaled by warriors in subsequent conflicts. This occurred partly because of their style of combat. Unlike other types of modern warfare, that pit huge armies and impersonal machines against each other, pilots conjured up images of gallant knights. Instead of picking up swords and fastening suits of armor, the pilots climbed into their aircraft and headed into the fray. As knights struck from their horses frequently faced death, so, too, did World

War I aviators stare at their demises should their aircraft be damaged. Newspaper reporters recited their heroics in glowing terms, much to the delight of enthralled readers in Germany, England, France, and the United States. Here one encountered true warfare of old, where foes charged each other and approached close enough to stare into one another's eyes. Since the men painted insignias on their aircraft, pilots from both sides frequently knew the identity of the man they were attacking.

Most pilots felt an uplifting sense of exhilaration and freedom as they prowled the skies, searching for the enemy. German aviator Hans Buddecke claimed that the instant he swerved his airplane and charged at a foe was his most precious moment, and British pilot Sholto Douglas said, "As I twisted and turned and dived and zoomed and fired and was shot at, I sometimes found myself shouting absurd battle cries, and even singing at the top of my voice."[1]

The pilots received enormous publicity and attention back home, in some cases comparable to today's rock stars or sports legends. The public, fascinated by the thought of a man entering a flimsily constructed device and defending the nation's honor two or three miles high, swarmed the top pilots whenever they appeared in view. Magazines profiled their lives, and memoirs penned by the fliers soared to the best-seller lists. A book written by the most famous pilot of all, Germany's "Red Baron," Manfred von Richthofen, enjoyed best-selling status even in enemy England. Because of the in-

"I Couldn't Kill Him"

Chivalry in the skies depended on the man in the aircraft. Some, like England's Edward Mannock, killed with a vengeance. Others, like American gunner Gill Robb Wilson in the following story from Arthur Gordon's *American Heritage History of Flight*, possessed more compassion. One day he and pilot Jean Henin took to the air.

"We got into a dogfight over the Oise canal [in France]. I was firing to the rear. Suddenly I felt Henin beating me on the back, and I could hear him yelling, 'Here, over here! Fire, fire!'

I turned around, and there with his wings locked with ours was a German fighter pilot. I looked right down this German's throat. How in God's name he ever got there I don't know. I could touch the end of his wing.

I swung the guns on him, and the guy just sat there. He had a mustache. I can still see him. There were deep lines on his face, and he looked at me with a kind of resignation. I looked over those machine guns at that guy, and I couldn't kill him. He was too helpless.

Gradually, he drifted off. I said to Henin, 'I couldn't kill him.' He said, 'I'm glad you didn't.'"

tense dangers the pilots faced, famed author H. G. Wells suggested that British pilots be knighted by the king.

Top aviators got to fly the newest and fastest aircraft and received extra pay for their hazardous duty. While infantry soldiers wallowed in the mud and blood of the trenches, pilots returned from a few hours of battle to hot food and warm beds. What most disturbed the soldier on the ground, however, was the attention an airman received from adoring females. One French pilot chided his infantry friend, "Ah, the girls, old man, once you've got those wings on your sleeve you can have as many as you want."[2]

Every aviator basked in the adulation, but pilots known as "aces" received special attention. Most nations followed the French system, which considered a man an ace after downing his fifth enemy aircraft, while Germany required its pilots to lodge ten kills. All countries stipulated that eyewitnesses had to verify the kill, and that the downed aircraft could not land in its own territory.

A common bond united pilots of all nations, forged by sharing risks unique to their style of warfare. Planes, barely more than lightweight cloth stretched over metal air frames, could suddenly collapse during steep dives. Few pilots had to worry about parachutes failing to open, since they scorned their use as unreliable and as providing an excuse to leave the aircraft too soon. Instead, pilots faced the unthinkable alternative of either going down with the plane in a blazing inferno or leaping to their death. Not surprisingly, many opted for the latter.

Again similar to knights living under the code of chivalry, pilots worried lest their reputations as aggressive fighters be criticized. A French aviator once had to withdraw from battle when his machine gun jammed. Worried that the Germans would consider him a coward, later that day he flew over a German airfield and delivered a note challenging one man to an aerial contest. No one accepted his offer, but the pilot had redeemed his honor.

Chivalry existed to such an extent that airmen dropped messages on enemy airfields informing them of any enemy airman's death or dropping wreaths in honor of slain opponents. A German aviator started the practice early in the war when he flew over Paris and dropped a note asking that the families of four captured French airmen be informed the men were safe.

"You Today, Me Tomorrow"

Above all, the pilots never forgot that their purpose in battle was to kill. They may honor a foe and drink a toast to their shared dangers, but once in the sky they concentrated on killing one another. French ace Alfred Heurtaux discussed the downing of a German aircraft and its two occupants as though he were describing an afternoon sporting match. "First I killed the pilot. The observer was in the rear shooting at me with a machine gun. When the pilot was killed, the observer held up his two hands [in surrender] and I remember his expression, the fear in his eyes. I will remember it always. He was killed in the crash—he had no chance to escape."[3]

Death constantly hovered over each man, producing ulcers and sleeplessness. Aviators lived in the present instead of dwelling on a future that might never arrive. Italian pilots fatalistically approached each battle with the saying, "You today, me tomorrow,"[4] and a British study concluded that pilots lost their effectiveness—through death, injury, or exhaustion—in battle after only two and one-half months. Pilots carried in their pockets an

"Don't Feel Sorry for Me"

Since death stared at them each day, before heading into battle some pilots wrote letters to parents or other loved ones to be opened in the event of their death. One French pilot penned a letter to his fellow airmen, which was read on July 28, 1918, after he perished in combat. The letter, taken from Lee Kennett's *The First Air War, 1914–1918*, illustrates some aviators' casual attitude toward death.

> Since you are reading this, you know that I've cashed in my chips. My turn was a long time coming. In the end it was bound to come. Well, too bad. Don't feel sorry for me, there's no need. Just remember that I tried to do my job as best I could, and that I did it in the best of company, among comrades who set me a good example. These few lines are just to thank you and to say goodbye.

Soldiers pay a respectful visit to wreckage from a Royal Air Force Sopwith Camel fighter.

array of lucky medallions or mementos from home, and superstitious actions dominated behavior. For instance, some men refused to wish one another luck, while others would glance away as an aircraft spun to the ground rather than see the men aboard perish.

Alfred Heurtaux headed into battle as a young man, but quickly lost the sense of exuberance. As he remembered, "I was twenty-three years old. All of us were very young. Everyone was in good spirits [at the war's start], and there was a feeling of camaraderie. It was like a sport. But in 1917, when several were killed, the mood changed. None of the old pilots was left."[5]

Among those who failed to survive was a twenty-five-year-old German flier. Before his death he established a reputation for such expert piloting and superb marksmanship that his name was known to all. Manfred von Richthofen, the Red Baron, dominated the skies for much of the war.

Chapter 1

The Red Baron

Talented fliers came from every nation during World War I, but the individual who garnered the most praise from friend and foe alike was Germany's indomitable Manfred von Richthofen (pronounced Rick-toe-fen), nicknamed the Red Baron. Combining superior flying skill with accurate aim, Richthofen literally flew circles around many of his opponents. For much of the war he occupied the top spot among aviators, a post he surrendered only in death.

Early Life

The most renowned aviator to emerge from World War I was born on May 2, 1892, in Breslau, Prussia, to wealthy parents. The landowners traced their family nobility to the seventeenth century, when Germany's revered leader Frederick the Great elevated the Richthofens to the lofty class and granted them extensive land in Silesia, a part of Prussia. As a result, Richthofen males gained the title of baron.

The oldest of three boys, the athletic Manfred quickly showed skill with horses. Most days, sitting erect in the saddle, he dashed through the thick forests that populated the family estate, his blond hair flying in the wind. Like other males of his family, Manfred became an expert hunter and soon accumulated an extensive collection of animal heads as testament to his prowess. He frequently told friends that he excelled at hunting because he loved the challenge of pitting his skills one-on-one against that of the animal.

A military career appeared to be Manfred's future, the expected occupation for the oldest son of a German family in those days. Manfred's father, a strict disciplinarian, had been an officer until an ear infection caused a hearing loss that led to his retirement. The proud Prussian had jumped into a cold river to save a drowning soldier, and then refused to change out of his wet clothes until he had completed his regular duties.

As the family's oldest son, Manfred von Richthofen was destined for a military career.

This sense of duty infused each male in the Richthofen household, even when the task lacked appeal, and before he entered his teenage years Manfred had to enroll in a military school. "As a little boy of eleven I entered the Cadet Corps," he later wrote in his memoirs. "I was not particularly eager to become a Cadet, but my father wished it. So my wishes were not consulted."[6]

Richthofen, more accustomed to galloping though forests and hunting animals, hated the regimen imposed by the Cadet Corps. He loved sports, especially soccer and gymnastics, but fared poorly in acade-

mic subjects. "I never was good at learning things. I did just enough work to pass. The consequence was that my teachers did not think overmuch of me."[7]

Richthofen managed to complete his studies, and then attended the Royal Military Academy and the Air Academy in Berlin. Still uninterested in the academies, where he had to focus on classwork, Richthofen eagerly jumped at the opportunity to join the unit to which his father had belonged, the First Regiment of Uhlans, in 1911. What made the move more enticing was that the Uhlans was a group of highly regarded cavalry. Richthofen would be back on a horse again.

Into the World War

Three years later, World War I cast much of Europe into conflict. Richthofen and the Uhlans, stationed in the eastern portion of Germany, received orders to drive into Poland to check any potential Russian advance through that nation. Eager to experience combat—Richthofen claimed that "It is in the blood of every German to rush to meet the enemy"[8]—he and the Uhlans scouted in front of German infantry to uncover Russian positions.

Richthofen soon realized his wish. While resting in the village of Kielce in present-day Poland, Richthofen and his comrades had to disperse when a much larger contingent of Russian cavalry unexpectedly appeared. Each man headed to the woods to elude capture or death. Some failed and were never seen again, but most safely returned to friendly zones that same day. Richthofen, however, had trouble shaking the enemy and had to remain in hiding for a few days. When he finally rejoined his unit, everyone stared at him as if they had seen a ghost, for by that time all had assumed he was dead. The military had even notified his parents that their son had died in battle.

Mother and father rejoiced at the good news of his survival, but elsewhere in the widespread Richthofen clan sorrow reigned. In the war's opening months, six of Manfred's cousins, all in the cavalry, perished.

The Uhlans then headed to France for Germany's massive 1914 drive into that country. Again scouting for the infantry, Richthofen rode ahead to purposely draw enemy fire, which gave the Uhlans an opportunity to determine the strength and location of French forces.

This dangerous tactic almost cost him his life. One time the Uhlans followed a set of French horse tracks through the woods when the tracks suddenly disappeared in a confined section. Richthofen later recalled, "To the right of our narrow path was a steep rocky wall many yards high. To the left, a narrow rivulet, and at the further side a meadow, 50 yards wide, surrounded by barbed wire."[9]

Suddenly the forest came alive with gunfire. From three sides French bullets ripped into the Uhlan ranks. Riders fell from their horses while officers tried to rally their men. Almost totally hemmed in, the Uhlans had no choice but to turn back and ride along the narrow path that led them to the ambush, all the time subject to French gunfire. Many Uhlans died or were taken prisoner, but Richthofen and a handful of others successfully rode out of the trap. "If I live through this war, I will have more luck than sense,"[10] gushed the grateful Richthofen after avoiding injury.

By fall of 1914 the fighting along the western front plunged into trench warfare. Rather than a war of movement, in which cavalry played a prominent role, the opposing armies settled into a static war in which neither side moved more than a handful of yards or miles at a time. Soldiers spent weeks

"A More Intimate and Personal Affair"

Aerial combat in World War I differed in many ways from that of World War II. One of the main differences was the proximity of opposing airmen as they engaged in battle—pilots maneuvered close to their quarry to get a better chance at shooting them down. Charles J. Biddle, an American pilot, describes the phenomenon in the foreword to French ace René Fonck's memoirs, *Ace of Aces.*

> Perhaps the thing that will impress the latter generation most will be the distances at which air fighting took place in the early days. Nearly all air combats in World War I which ended in victory for one or the other were fought at under 100 yards, and most of these at about 40 to 60 yards. The minimum was when it became necessary to pull out to avoid a collision. None of these long-range encounters at hundreds of yards, with electrically controlled sights and multiple machine guns and cannons, which make accuracy possible at such distances. It was a much more intimate and personal affair.

and months in the same trenches, attacking the enemy and defending against enemy attacks directed at them.

With little work for the cavalry in such a situation, Richthofen spent the next few months as a supply officer. The active young officer considered the move a demotion and dashed a flurry of letters to his commander requesting a transfer to the recently formed air service. Richthofen knew the aviation section needed good observers in each aircraft who could spot enemy concentrations below, and figuring that the duty shared common features with his cavalry work, he believed he could do well. Besides, anything would be better than distributing food.

"I have not gone to war to collect cheese and eggs," he wrote his superior officer, "but for much another reason."[11] The young man's persistence finally produced results, and by spring 1915 he transferred to the German Flying Corps.

First an Observer

The most famous ace of World War I first served in the air as an observer in a two-seater plane. While another man piloted the craft, Richthofen studied the land below for signs of enemy movement and positions.

He instantly fell in love with his new occupation, as if he and the sky were one. Soaring through the air at speeds approaching one hun-

dred miles per hour reminded him of riding his horse at top speed through his beloved Silesian forests. After his initial training flight, Richthofen wrote

The men [below] looked ridiculously small. The houses seemed to come out of a child's toy box. Everything seemed pretty. Cologne [a town in Germany] was in the background. The cathedral looked like a little toy. It was a glorious feeling to be so high above the earth, to be master of the air. I didn't care a bit where I was, and I felt extremely sorry

Richthofen (center) and a comrade in front of his famous red triplane.

when my pilot thought it was time to go down again. I was full of enthusiasm, and would have liked to be sitting in an aeroplane all day long. I counted the hours to the next start.[12]

Richthofen spent three months as an observer on the eastern front before being shifted to France in August 1915. Though he climbed into an aircraft almost every day, he quickly tired of what he considered the inactive role of observer. He lusted after the pilot's seat, where he would have control of both the craft's direction and its machine guns. If he were to engage in a hunt, he wanted to be able to kill, not simply observe.

Off to Training

Richthofen sent a barrage of requests to superiors to be admitted to the pilot's program, and since Germany needed good pilots his wishes materialized. Richthofen soon learned that flying an airplane and riding a horse were far different tasks. That first training flight as a pilot humbled the fledgling aviator—he could not shout loud enough to be heard by the accompanying flight instructor, the wind blew a piece of paper out of his hand that he intended to give his companion, his flying helmet slipped off, and he buttoned his jacket improperly. All this occurred before he even left the ground.

Surprisingly, Richthofen earned low marks for his flying skills. He crashed one aircraft while attempting to land and failed not only his first solo flight, but also his first and second attempts at the written exam.

Fortunately, Germany needed trained pilots so desperately that Richthofen was not dropped from the program.

If he could not display expertise behind the controls, at least Richthofen proved that he would not shrink from a challenge. When his instructor informed him on October 10, 1915, that Richthofen was to fly alone for the first time, Richthofen masked his apprehension and stepped to the aircraft. "I must say I felt like replying, 'I am afraid.' But this is a word which should never be used by a man who defends his country. Therefore, whether I liked it or not, I had to swallow it and get into the machine."[13]

Richthofen performed well enough that in December 1915 he officially became a pilot and was sent to the western front, but his lackluster performance in training school caused superiors to hold him out of combat for a time. Devastated, Richthofen wrote his mother in January 1916, "I have not flown, not even once. I seem to be making no progress. I should love to be at the front right now. I think there is so much going on there."[14]

To the Front

Richthofen finally received his chance to head off to battle in the spring of 1916, but as the pilot of a two-man observation plane that sported just one machine gun, in the observer's cockpit. Eager to shoot at the enemy himself, Richthofen attached a gun to the upper wing of his aircraft so he could reach it and quickly downed two French planes. Because the victims fell behind French lines and thus could not be confirmed as kills, Richthofen did not receive credit for either triumph.

In June 1916, Richthofen's unit headed to the eastern front for bombing and reconnaissance duties, but this rather sedate occupation lacked appeal. Richthofen, so accustomed to the thrill of the hunt, wanted to battle one-on-one in his own fighter aircraft against an opponent.

A noted German pilot named Oswald Boelcke (pronounced Bulka) handed Richthofen his ticket to fame. Given the job of forming an elite air unit, in August 1916, Boelcke visited the eastern front in search of promising pilots. Even though Richthofen lacked an impressive flying record, he hoped the prominent officer would select him for his squadron.

Boelcke loved Richthofen's enthusiasm for flying and his desire to engage the enemy, and decided that those factors overcame the aviator's shortcomings in training. Boelcke sat down with the younger man and asked, "For some real fighting, Baron, would you care to come with me to the Somme [a region of intense fighting in France]?" Richthofen readily agreed and headed to France for a span he labeled as "the finest time of my life."[15]

Richthofen returns from a reconnaissance flight over the western front.

With Boelcke

Richthofen gained his greatest experience in the few months he flew with Boelcke, who helped raise German airpower to supremacy on the western front. Before 1916 the Allies controlled the air, but Field Marshal Paul von Hindenburg, the chief of the German general staff, created pursuit squadrons called *Jagdstaffeln* [fighter squadrons] to counter that domination. Hindenburg's tactics worked, for in September and October,

German pilots shot down 211 Allied aircraft compared to the loss of only 39 German planes to break the Allied stranglehold over the Somme.

Boelcke's squadron garnered the most notoriety. Boelcke emphasized that his fighter pilots should attack a target from below and behind, since that was where an enemy pilot would have the most difficulty seeing them, and he took them into the air at every opportunity.

Boelcke "shot one or two Englishmen for breakfast every day,"[16] enthused Richthofen, who adored his mentor. The elder Boelcke reciprocated the feelings, for whenever anyone asked which of his talented pilots would become the best, he pointed to Richthofen.

Richthofen gained his first kill on September 17, 1916, when Boelcke led Richthofen and three other pilots against eight British bombers escorted by six fighters. Boelcke cautiously maneuvered his men into position before giving the signal to attack. On his first attempt Richthofen passed too close to a British fighter, which just missed pumping a round of machine gun bullets into his craft. Then he remembered Boelcke's advice about attacking from behind and below, approached another enemy fighter from the rear, took aim, and killed both observer and pilot. Richthofen followed the stricken aircraft as it plummeted to the ground. Then he landed and ran to the plane while German soldiers removed the bodies of two British airmen. He had registered his first official kill.

A Legacy Begins

That night Richthofen ordered the first of what would be a lengthy line of silver cups from a Berlin jeweler to honor his kills. The two-inch-tall cups bore the date and type of aircraft downed and occupied a place of honor in his family home.

"During my whole life I have not found a happier hunting ground than in the course of the Somme Battle," wrote Richthofen in his memoirs. "In the morning, as soon as I had got up, the first Englishman arrived, and the last disappeared only long after sunset."[17] Flying the fastest, most maneuverable aircraft produced by Germany, the Albatros D.II, Richthofen, Boelcke, and the rest of the squadron outclassed their British and French opponents

Disregard for Death

Death and injury were constant companions to World War I pilots. They saw fellow aviators succumb to enemy bullets, to malfunctions, or to pilot error, and thus grew fatalistic about their own chances of survival.

One way to deal with the intense pressure was to joke about it. The words of the following tune, sung by pilots as they hoisted toasts to one another, provides a good example. It comes from *They Fought for the Sky* by Quentin Reynolds.

The young aviator went stunting,
And as 'neath the wreckage he lay,
To the mechanics assembled around him,
These last parting words did he say.

Take the cylinders out of my kidneys,
The connecting rod out of my brain
From the small of my back take the crankshaft,
And assemble the engine again.

and grabbed air supremacy over the western front.

One of Richthofen's most famous encounters took place on November 11, 1916, when he battled Britain's legendary Maj. Lanoe George Hawker. Richthofen was flying alone when Hawker approached from the rear. The two aces then engaged in a deadly dogfight, each trying to maneuver his craft to be on the other's tail. As excited soldiers watched from the trenches below, Richthofen and Hawker circled as many as fifty times at varying altitudes to achieve proper firing position, but neither succeeded.

Hawker then executed a series of tricky loops to shake Richthofen. When that failed, he dropped to three hundred feet above the ground and started zigzagging, but the persistent German pilot, enjoying the exhilaration of the hunt, peppered the British plane with bullets and killed Hawker with a shot to the head. Richthofen landed near the crashed airplane, retrieved Hawker's machine gun, and placed it at the front of his tent as a war trophy. From then on, Richthofen grabbed souvenirs from his downed aircraft—serial numbers off the plane's side, pistols, propeller fragments, or any portion of the aircraft—and sent them home to be placed in his room.

He may have enjoyed comparing aerial combat with hunting, but Richthofen could see that the two stood worlds apart. Danger constantly dogged the aviators, and Richthofen understood that many would not see the war's end. One time the upper wing of his plane shattered and forced Richthofen into a hasty landing, and almost every day the absence of a fellow pilot reminded the men that, in this hunt, the quarry could shoot back.

"In the last six weeks," he wrote his mother, "we have had, of our twelve pilots, six dead and one wounded, while two have suffered a complete nervous collapse. Yesterday I brought down my seventh shortly after I had accounted for my sixth. The ill luck of the others has not yet affected my nerves."[18]

Death granted no favors to men of renown. On October 28, 1916, Boelcke's aircraft broke a wing when it brushed against another German plane during a battle. The pilot, with forty kills to his credit, fell to his death in the freakiest of accidents. British pilots flew over the French town of Cambrai on the day of Boelcke's funeral and dropped wreaths on the procession, proclaiming their German foe to be a gallant and chivalrous competitor. Richthofen, who carried Boelcke's many decorations on a pillow during the procession, told his mother that the service compared favorably to those given reigning monarchs.

The Baron Becomes a Leader

Life dramatically altered for Richthofen at the start of 1917. He became Germany's leading living flying ace when he recorded his sixteenth downed enemy aircraft, and he was handed his own squadron, *Jagdstaffel 11*, to command. Richthofen was unhappy about leaving Boelcke's unit.

To boost morale and mock the enemy, Richthofen's unit Jagdstaffel 11 *(pictured)— painted their aircraft bright colors, earning the name "flying circus" from British airmen.*

"I must say I was annoyed. I had learnt to work so well with my comrades of Boelcke's squadron, and now I had to begin all over again working hand in hand with different people. It was a beastly nuisance."[19]

Despite his feelings, Richthofen quickly asserted his authority. He molded the young men in his own image, instructing his pilots how to engage the enemy and give themselves the greatest chances of survival. He covered a list of items that he felt ensured success—how to best position their aircraft for attack; to avoid attacking observation balloons, which were tethered to the ground and always heavily guarded by anti-aircraft guns and enemy fighter aircraft; to allow the opponent to make the first move,

then decide whether to engage or pull back depending on how skilled the foe appeared to be; and to let off a burst of fire while far away to distract the enemy's attention and rattle his nerves. He taught the men that victory would go to the man who remained calmer and who used his head in tight situations, and that one should aim at the man rather than the machine.

"Never shoot holes in a machine. Aim for the man and don't miss him. If you are fighting a two-seater, get the observer first;

until you have silenced the gun don't bother about the pilot."[20] The bodies of Richthofen's victims usually had bullet holes in them, indicating that Richthofen followed his own advice.

After each flight, Richthofen gathered his men to discuss what went right or wrong. If he thought one pilot tried to be too fancy in the sky or attempted to show off his skills, Richthofen's harsh rebuke usually was enough to halt the offending practice. Any man who properly executed his duty and proved his courage under fire received the baron's most loyal support; any who failed to measure up quickly departed. Another German ace explained that Richthofen "judges a man by what he accomplishes. He who passes this judgment, he backs all the way. Whoever fails, he drops without batting an eyelash. Whoever shows lukewarm on a sortie [is not aggressive in battle] has to leave the group— the same day."[21]

The Flying Circus is Born

To instill pride in the unit and to taunt the enemy, Richthofen painted his own aircraft bright red. This way, everyone in the air and on the ground would know who prowled the skies. His men imitated him, and soon such a wild assortment of colorful German machines assembled for battle that British airmen started calling the unit the "flying circus." Pilots hopped into aircraft that had green wings and yellow noses, silver wings with gold noses, red bodies with green wings, light blue bodies and red wings.

Since Richthofen received the best pilots and the fastest aircraft, *Jagdstaffel 11* became feared by the enemy and admired at home. To combat this threat, the British produced newer aircraft and assembled a special unit of expert fliers whose task was to hunt the Red Baron. A large cash award was offered to the pilot who killed Richthofen, leading the German to humorously wonder whether he could collect the money if he, instead, shot down the entire British squadron.

Richthofen came close to accomplishing such a feat. By April 23, 1917, Richthofen recorded his forty-seventh kill and assumed first place among all German aviators, dead or alive. In that month alone German pilots shot down seventy-five British aircraft, most notched by men of the flying circus, which included the baron's brother, Lothar.

No pilot could afford to relax his vigilance, even when battles seemed to go his way, since danger always lurked. In March 1917 bullets tore into Richthofen's gas tank and forced him into a fast landing. On July 6, 1917, as he patrolled near the Belgian town of Ypres, a bullet slashed a three-inch cut across Richthofen's scalp and nearly knocked him unconscious. Richthofen was able to land his airplane, but passed out before German ground troops rushed to his aid. When they arrived and found the baron covered in blood, the German soldiers feared the ace was dead, but a fast inspection proved Richthofen to be in good shape.

Richthofen joked that his thick skull had saved him from death, but as the war went into its final year he had fewer reasons to laugh. The injury and the continual grind of battle sapped his energy, and after each mission Richthofen returned to his tent and collapsed. He avoided the other men and spent hours by himself. His brother and the other pilots noticed that Richthofen seemed obsessed with death, especially by fire, and talked of all the British and French airmen he had sent to fiery ends.

Though altered by war, Richthofen continued to excel. Some days he registered two or three kills, and by April 20, 1918, his total

Recovering from a head wound in July 1917, Richthofen (pictured with his father) became quite solitary and dispirited near the war's end.

had soared to eighty victims. Whereas earlier in the war Richthofen had delighted in each victory, he now found little solace. "I am in wretched spirits after every battle," he wrote home. "When I set foot on the ground again I go to my quarters and do not want to see anyone or hear anything."[22]

"Don't You Think I'll Come Back?"

Although he did not realize it, the eightieth was to be Richthofen's final kill. The next day as Richthofen climbed into his aircraft for another mission, a young pilot asked for his autograph. Richthofen, who planned to take leave soon and return home to hunt with friends, smiled and asked, "What's the matter? Don't you think I'll come back?"[23]

He did not. Twenty miles away the men of British Squadron 209, including Capt. Roy Brown, climbed into their planes. At 10:45 A.M., Brown spotted fifteen German aircraft over the Somme River, and he and Lt. Wilfred R. May dove to attack. A jammed gun forced May to leave, but Richthofen doggedly pursued him. May saw the bright red plane and attempted to evade his illustrious opponent, but Richthofen closed the gap. As the German prepared to fire a burst into May, Brown crept from behind and punctured the red aircraft with an accurate stream of bullets. Brown later recalled, "A full burst ripped into the side of the airplane. The pilot turned around and looked back. I saw the glint of his eyes behind the big goggles, then he collapsed in the seat."[24]

Richthofen's plane continued for another mile before crashing near a trench

"No Satisfaction in Victory"

After shooting down Richthofen, Captain Roy Brown visited the tent in which the Baron's body had been placed. Though he had just been credited with killing the war's top ace, Brown felt no sense of accomplishment. As recorded in Ezra Bowen's 1980 book, *Knights of the Air,* Brown felt sadness instead.

He looked so small to me, so delicate. His cap had been removed. Blond, silk-soft hair, like that of a child, fell from the broad high forehead. His face, particularly peaceful, had an expression of gentleness and goodness, of refinement. I did not feel like a victor.

British soldiers inspect the remains of Richthofen's airplane after British captain Roy Brown shot him down in combat.

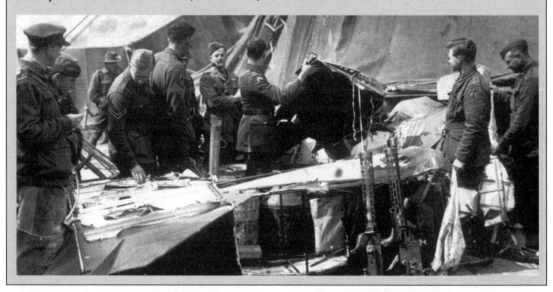

occupied by Australian troops. The Allied soldiers found Richthofen's lifeless body slumped forward, blood pouring from his mouth and his head leaning against one of the machine guns he had so ably used.

The next day a British aircraft dropped a note over a German airfield informing the Germans of Richthofen's death and of his burial by Allied soldiers. An honor guard of thirteen Australian soldiers, marched to the cemetery with their rifles reversed in a sign of honor, escorted the body as it was moved through the countryside to a place of burial near Bertangles in northeastern France. With Allied aviators—his combat foes—as pallbearers and with wreaths covering his casket, Manfred von Richthofen was buried eleven days before his twenty-sixth birthday.

The news stunned Germany. One top officer claimed that Richthofen's death was equal to losing thirty infantry divisions. After the war his body was exhumed and taken to Berlin for burial with full military honors.

Chapter 2

The Child as Killer

Many top aces of World War I had to deal with the tensions produced by opposing emotions. While they loved the thrill of the chase and the excitement of soaring into the heavens, they shuddered at the human cost of their ventures. Even though they spoke of downing "machines," they realized that inside each aircraft breathed one or two human beings, and that haunted all but the most callous. Great Britain's Albert Ball typified these feelings, but he added another dimension not usually seen in other pilots—rarely have the qualities of the child been so lethally combined with those of the killer.

Youth in Nottingham

Nottingham, England, resonates in history with the sound of arrows thudding into trees and with merry men, led by legendary Robin Hood, fighting for their freedom against a dastardly sheriff. The region, however, produced more than one significant figure. Another favorite son battled Germans, not the sheriff, and he fired bullets rather than arrows.

Albert Ball Jr., the man who would for a time hold the title of England's top World War I ace, was born in Nottingham on August 14, 1896, the second of three children. His father, Albert Sr., successfully turned a lucrative real estate business into a career as a politician, first serving the region as a councillor and then as lord mayor of Nottingham. Ball's father accumulated enough money at real estate that he could eventually move his burgeoning family into a larger house surrounded by verdant gardens.

Ball's nervous energy and desire to constantly be involved in activity aped his father's tendencies. He learned to be an expert marksman at an early age by shooting at tin cans. Ball could also spend hours tinkering with old engines. He loved to figure out how something worked, usually by purchasing an old worn-out engine at low cost, dismantling it and spreading the pieces out on the ground, then carefully reassem-

Albert Ball enlisted in the army to serve Britain during World War I.

bling it to see if he could get it to work better. When the new invention of radio appeared, Albert enthusiastically picked up a set and became one of the few skilled operators in the area.

The youth did not shine academically, either at Nottingham High School or when he boarded at Trent College in nearby Long Eaton. He excelled, however, in those areas that interested him, and not surprisingly those fell in the mechanical arena. Figuring that he had a bright future in the electrical industry, where he hoped to devise ways to bring power to homes in outlying regions, Ball took extra mathematics and technical classes.

Ball also exhibited a softer side, and as a result he and his mother, Harriet, developed a fast bond. It was not that Albert's mother favored him over younger brother Cyril or older sister Lois; it was simply that they shared things in common. Ball relaxed with his hobby of photography, by playing the violin, or by working in the family garden—all habits his mother found more attractive than his mechanical side. Harriet also loved the fact that when Albert was away at Trent College, he wrote her a letter almost every day.

Knowing his energy and love for the occupation, Ball probably would have succeeded in the electrical industry had not World War I come along. He started a small business after graduating from Trent College and appeared to be on his way to establishing a thriving occupation until August 1914, when most of Europe descended into the chaos of war.

Choosing Duty over Desire

Ball hated to abandon his fledgling concern, but like his father he believed that a man had a duty to help his nation in time of danger. As a youth, Ball had his picture taken while standing in front of a mammoth wooden door bearing the carved inscription of Lord Nelson's famed words, "England expects that every man will do his duty," so he became one of the first young men from Nottingham to enlist in the army.

He was placed with a unit of men from the area called the Sherwood Foresters and stationed near an airfield in the south of England for training. Eager to see action in

France, Ball was disappointed when the Foresters received orders to concentrate to the east of London to forestall a then-feared German invasion of England.

"I am very disappointed just now," he wrote home. "I have just sent five boys to France and I hear they will be in the firing line on Monday. It is just my luck to be unable to go."[25] Like many other young men in those heady first days of war, Ball could barely contain his excitement at acquiring a taste of combat. And, like the others, Ball would soon realize the horror that lurked on the battlefield.

During training, the mechanically inclined Ball could not help but notice the airfield close by. To make room for flying lessons, Ball arose at 3 A.M. three times each week, rode a bicycle to the airfield, practiced flying, then returned to his unit for a full day's duty. Somehow he survived seven crashes. He wrote his father that "When I got up to 800 feet my control went wrong, and I came crashing down, smashing the bottom of the machine in. I was not hurt. I had lots of time to think what was taking place, in fact it made me laugh, although I thought it rotten to smash the machine."[26]

Ball's persistence paid dividends, however, and by October 1915 he qualified for his pilot's certificate. Hoping to be sent across the Channel to France, Ball requested a transfer to the Royal Flying Corps. In February 1916 an impatient Ball finally received the news he longed to hear—he was ordered to join a squadron of British pilots posted in France.

"Some Strange Power Was There"

Ball joined No. 13 Squadron in France at a difficult time for the British. Sporting faster, more powerful aircraft and accurate antiaircraft fire, the Germans were enjoying a huge advantage over the English. The result was not surprising—destroyed British airplanes littered the French countryside for miles around the fighting areas.

Despite the danger, Ball reveled in his new duty. As pilot of a two-seater observer aircraft, his task was to fly the plane over enemy positions while his companion photographed the trenches below and made notes of German defenses. The fearless Ball, bored with such unadventurous

The Sherwood Foresters

Albert Ball eventually wound up in the air, but his mind and thoughts never strayed far from his comrades in the Sherwood Foresters, who endured some of the worst carnage the war in Europe produced. On July 1, 1916 the men received orders to take Gommecourt from the Germans. Advancing across the muddy fields young men, many of whom were personal friends of Ball, fell in swaths before German artillery and machine gun fire. The commanding officer and his aide were killed in the opening moments, and only twelve men reached the German wire.

Survivors waited until dark to crawl from shell holes and hiding places back to friendly lines. Ball's former unit started July 1 with 627 men—less than 130 survived. Overall, fifty-seven thousand British soldiers were killed or wounded just this first day of the Somme offensive. Ball's fatalistic attitude about dying, which increased as the war progressed, and his frequent referrals to the Sherwood Foresters indicated the importance he placed on what happened to his buddies below.

flying, usually managed to locate a German airplane for a dogfight, even if it meant leaving the other British fliers. The young man quickly established a reputation as a daredevil.

Ball felt that his skills as an aviator were being wasted and requested a transfer to a unit of single-seater fighters. Whenever he could, he jumped into No. 13's sole single-seater to practice shooting its machine gun and to prepare for the time when he would be master of his own aircraft.

He received his wish in May 1916 by being posted to No. 11 Squadron, a unit employing the sleek Nieuport single-seater machine. Ball embarrassingly almost shot himself down in his first flight when the synchronization mechanism controlling the passage of machine gun bullets through the plane's propeller failed. Ball fired a burst at an enemy craft but hit little besides his own propeller.

Ball believed that in war the highest mission was to kill the enemy. Most British pilots flew in groups, but Ball hated flying in formation and usually abandoned his cohorts to fly over German territory alone and seek an engagement with a willing adversary.

The young pilot, whose face reminded observers of a child, hardly looked the image of a military officer. He never wore goggles or a flying helmet since they restricted his head movements in the sky and chafed the back of his neck. Instead of the spit-and-polish look, Ball's uniform sported oil stains from his continual tinkering with the engine, and his boots contained a heavy layer

When assigned to the No. 11 Squadron, Ball flew a Nieuport 11, also known as "Bebe."

of mud and dirt. But no one who looked at the youth doubted his abilities.

"To look at Albert Ball he appeared still a boy, short, hair unkempt and shy-looking" said a fellow airman. "It was only when those dark piercing eyes would turn and rest on yours did you realize that some strange power was there—some power that made him in some way different to other men."[27]

Relentless

Flying to the motto of "Attack everything!" Ball scoured the skies like a hungry lion seeking prey. Pilots had orders to fly above seven thousand feet so German machine guns and rifle fire from the trenches could do no harm, but Ball fearlessly pursued German aircraft even when they dropped to within a few hundred feet of the ground. If a superior questioned him about his dangerous tactics, Ball replied that at least the enemy wasted machine gun bullets trying to knock him down.

Some pilots admired Ball's reckless tactics while others swore that he carried a death wish. Ball usually fired a few shots at a group of German planes to break it up, then focused on the nearest machine to destroy it. In a move that required steely nerves and split-second timing, he loved to let an opponent approach from behind, wait until his instincts told him the German was about to open fire, then bank in a sharp turn to get

Ball, with the nose and propeller from his airplane, was known for his reckless flying and risky fighting tactics.

on the German's tail and shoot him down. At other times Ball pretended to be attacking from above, then would quickly drop below the target and riddle it with bullets as he veered back and forth from no more than ten yards underneath. The scariest part of this, he always claimed, was the danger that the German plane would plummet directly onto his own.

His most frightening tactic was to charge directly toward a German airplane in

Ball's first official kill on June 25, 1916, involved an observation balloon like the one shown here.

a head-on attack. He figured that no German would be foolish enough to accept the death-defying risk and pull back at the last moment, thus offering a tempting target for Ball's machine guns. The Germans became so aware of Ball's audacity that one British general joked that he would paint Ball's name in huge letters on a board and place the board near the front lines to scare the Germans.

Ball could execute these moves at minimal risk because his amazing eyesight allowed him to spot the enemy before they could locate him, and his mechanical abilities enabled him to improve his aircraft to give him more of an edge. For instance, Ball altered his machine gun mount so he could fire the gun in a more upward angle than other pilots, he rigged the plane's controls so that the plane could briefly fly itself, allowing him to use both hands on his ma-

chine gun, and he was the first flier to attach a mirror so he could see behind without having to turn his head. In addition, Ball shot with uncanny accuracy, just as he had as a schoolchild aiming at tin cans.

Ball wrote of his outings in letters home to his family. When his father mentioned the family's fears concerning Albert's safety, Ball replied that unless his parents and siblings stopped worrying so much, he would stop sending them informative letters and mail brief, boring accounts instead.

The War's Top Ace

Ball's tactics produced results. His first official kill—an observation balloon—came on

June 25, 1916. Seven days later he shot down his first airplane, and by August 22 the skilled pilot had eleven kills.

Each mission featured hazards of its own. One time in the summer of 1916 he attacked an observation balloon eight miles into German territory but missed with every bullet. Disgusted by his poor shooting, Ball returned to his airfield, reloaded, flew back to the site for a second foray, and sent the balloon down in flames. In the attack, though, German bullets hit Ball's engine and reduced his power. This forced Ball to fly low to the ground, making him an appealing target for German gunners for eight miles. He safely returned to base, pried one of the enemy bullets out of his aircraft, and sent it home as a souvenir. For his bravery Ball received the Military Cross.

Ball was shot down on at least six different occasions, but always escaped serious harm. Flying near the French town of Cambrai in August 1916, Ball spotted a group of Germans and dove to break up the formation. He quickly shot down two planes, but the others caught Ball in a crossfire. With a damaged airplane and out of ammunition, Ball had little choice but to pull back. As he did, however, Ball pulled out his revolver and fired off a few rounds at the enemy pilots. Ball safely crash-landed the aircraft in British-held territory.

Ball's missions did not always involve hunting. One time he volunteered to fly a spy behind German lines and land him at a prearranged spot. Little went right, as Ball explained in his account. Shortly after they crossed into German territory, three aircraft attacked. Normally Ball would have relished such a situation, but to make room for the spy and his luggage he had to remove his machine gun and could not return fire. Ball outran his pursuers until darkness provided some protection, but then ground fire and rockets lit up the area in an attempt to set his machine on fire. He recalled:

I really did think that the end had come. However, at last we found a landing place and we started down. Naturally everything had to be done quickly or we would have been caught. But we got down! Picture my temper when we landed. The damned spy would not get out. The [German airplanes] had frightened him and he would not risk it. There was nothing to do but get off again before the Huns came along and stopped us, so off we went. I went down three times again after this, but the rotter refused to do his part.[28]

Ball flew back to base and parted company with the reluctant spy.

From July to September in 1916, while horrendous ground fighting occurred near the Somme River, Ball shot down thirty German aircraft in equally furious aerial combat to become the war's leading ace. Rather than boast of his prowess, the shy Ball, acting more the schoolchild than the warrior, claimed that luck had handed him the victories rather than skill and courage.

31

An August 24, 1916, letter to his sister Lois sounds more like a report on a football game than the outcome of a deadly clash.

> Really, I am having too much luck for a boy. Met twelve Huns. No. 1 fight. I attacked and fired, bringing the machine down just outside a village. All crashed up. No. 2 fight. I attacked under the machine. Hun went down in flames. No. 3 fight. I attacked. Machine went down and crashed on a housetop.
>
> I only got hit 11 times in the wings, so I returned and got more ammunition. This time luck was not all on the spot. I was met by 14 Huns, about 15 miles over their side. My windscreen was hit in four places, mirror broken, the spar of the left wing broken, also engine ran out of petrol.
>
> Oh, la, la. Topping, isn't it?[29]

"I Am Beginning to Feel Like a Murderer"

The youth may have pictured battle encounters like a child describing a game, but on the inside, anguish slowly simmered. After completing a mission, instead of joining the other pilots in the unit's tent and relaxing with food, drink, and laughter, Ball headed to a separate tent he called his "dear old hut" and kept to himself. The humorless individual drew comfort from eating cakes sent by his mother, planting in a nearby garden cucumber and pea seeds mailed by his father, or playing his violin for hours at a time, particularly Austrian composer Franz Schu-

Battle Fatigue

Like many other pilots, as the war progressed Albert Ball suffered bouts of depression and exhaustion. Hesitation in battle and a fixation on death replaced the exuberance of the early days. Pilots took more dangerous risks than before, believing that their fate, whatever it might be, had already been determined and that whatever they did would not alter it. In his book *Knights of the Air*, Ezra Bowen quotes an American aviator who describes the feelings.

> You're tense at the beginning, then you reach the stage of being very cool and collected. You think you're a pretty good shot and a damned good pilot, and "it's going to take someone a hell of a lot better to shoot me down."

bert's *Unfinished Symphony*. The other fliers gave Ball his space, but they were upset at the young man's unusual ways and derisively labeled the loner's tent Ball's Hermitage.

Ball spent a great deal of time writing letters, particularly to his mother, in which he poured out his emotions. They show that Ball rode an emotional roller coaster about the tasks he performed in the war. The youthfulness in him yearned for decency and fun; the soldierly aspect required devotion to killing. A sense of duty to home and country propelled him to greater effort, but at the same time a feeling that he shared characteristics with murderers haunted him.

In one letter he explained to his mother why he served in the war. He fought

> because every boy who has loving people and a good home should go out and stand up for it. You think I have done

enough, but oh, no, there is not, or at least should not be, such a thought in such a war as this. I shall fight for you and come home for you, and God always looks after me and makes me strong; may He look after you also.[30]

In the same letter, he hinted that the strain of war lay heavy on his mind. "I am, indeed, looked after by God; but oh, I do get tired of always living to kill. I am beginning to feel like a murderer. Oh, won't it be nice when all this beastly killing is over, and we can just enjoy ourselves and not hurt anyone? I hate this game, but it is the only thing one must do just now."[31]

In other letters he admitted to family that he thought the German pilots were good opponents, and that "Nothing makes me feel more rotten than to see them go down."[32] However, he also wrote that he enjoyed strafing planes he had damaged to make sure the occupants were killed.

Although Ball may have held conflicting views, the British government and public had no such doubts. At first the British government hesitated to honor fighter pilots since it believed that such a move would make the contributions made by infantry in the trenches and by airmen in observation planes appear less significant. The policy changed in 1916, when potent German offensives in France tossed the British army on its heels. For instance, Ball's old outfit, the Sherwood Foresters, lost 80 percent of the unit in a single day's action trying to dislodge the Germans from the French village of Gommecourt. The public needed a hero now, and Ball fit the bill.

In October 1916, Ball received orders to return to England to train potential airmen. He hoped to relax from the rigors of combat, visit with his mother and father, and spend time in the family garden, but the British government had no intention of allowing Ball out of the public eye. King George V awarded him the Distinguished Service Order, the lord mayor of Sherwood hosted a formal luncheon in his honor, and Ball made frequent appearances for the British army. Even when Ball attempted to hide his identity with a shabby trench coat and sneak into town, everyone knew who he was.

Ball was awarded the Distinguished Service Order by the British army.

At one function the twenty-year-old Ball met seventeen-year-old Flora Young. Smitten with the girl, he asked her if she would like to take a ride in an airplane. The excited girl accepted, and the two began a friendship that turned into love. He wrote her every day, affectionately calling her "Bobs."

Ball felt uncomfortable away from the front, however. He had been in England no longer than a few days when he sent in his first request to be sent back to France, and eventually his pleading worked. In April 1917, Ball headed back to France as flight commander of No. 56 Squadron.

Return with a Vengeance

If Ball wanted action, he could not have chosen a better time to return. April 1917 produced such an appalling toll in injuries and death that pilots on both sides called it Bloody April. Ball jumped into the fray as if he had not missed a step, and within two weeks he added another ten kills to his total. He still preferred flying alone and fighting until he ran out of ammunition or was dangerously low on fuel, but those tactics placed him in more danger than they did a year ago. *Jastas* now roamed the skies—German killing squadrons that flew together in large numbers and entered battle as a unit rather than individually. The response called for greater care by British pilots, but Ball refused to abandon the techniques that had brought him such great success.

Since he now had a responsibility to lead, Ball usually flew patrols twice each day with his squadron, but in between he headed out alone to hunt for more Germans. One time while deep in enemy territory Ball attacked two German aircraft. The trio battled until the pilots ran out of ammunition, at which time the Germans headed back to base. Ball followed after them and dropped a note challenging the two men to duel the next day at the same time. The foolish move almost cost Ball his life, for when he appeared he found five German planes waiting for him. Three quickly flew behind Ball to cut him off from friendly lines, then closed in. Ball used every trick he knew to avoid the flurry of bullets that nipped at his aircraft, but realized that he could not avoid being damaged for long.

Ball spotted a large field and headed down as if to land. When his plane rolled to a stop, he slumped forward in the cockpit to make the German pilots think he had been hit, but kept his plane's engine idling. Three Germans left the scene while the other two descended to check out the wreck. As the two pilots climbed out of their planes, Ball gunned his engine and took off, leaving two startled Germans standing embarrassed in the middle of the field.

In another encounter with five hostile aircraft, Ball quickly shot down two planes before enemy bullets started to shred his wings. He purposely put his plane into a dangerous spin, then pulled out only yards above the ground. The German who followed Ball could not pull out of the spin and smashed into the field, and the final German hastened away after Ball shot down the fourth.

On May 2, 1917, Ball attacked two Germans. He quickly shot down one, then charged straight at the second in one of his favorite tactics. This time, though, the German seemed as determined as Ball and continued toward the British pilot. Ball watched his bullets tear into the German plane, but still the foe came on. As the distance between the two rapidly closed, Ball's airplane shuddered from a hit that threw engine oil into Ball's face. Blinded momentarily, Ball tensed and waited for the collision he expected, but nothing happened. When he wiped enough oil from his face to see, Ball noticed burning wreckage in a field below. Apparently the German had been hit by one of Ball's bullets, slumped against the control stick, and veered off at the final moment.

Ball continued to add to his grand score. On May 6 he recorded his forty-fourth victory, and nothing indicated that either his charmed life in the skies or his string of kills would end.

"I Am Feeling Very Old"

As happened to many pilots, constant battle in the skies took a mental toll on Ball. More often weary and depressed than before, Ball grew short-tempered and suffered from numbness. The invigorating excitement he once felt had been replaced with an aching desire to leave the fighting behind and flee to the welcome comfort of home and mother.

"I am feeling very old just now,"[33] he wrote his parents on May 3, 1917. The weariness made killing more burdensome than in

---

Exchanging Notes

One of the most intriguing portions of the aerial war was that while both sides tried to kill each other, they still maintained a semblance of decency and good manners. One manifestation appeared in the habit of communicating with the opposing side by flying to the enemy airfield and dropping notes. Most often the notes indicated that one of their own had been shot down and killed or taken prisoner. Sometimes it took the form of the following 1915 challenge to a duel, reprinted by Lee Kennett in his book, *The First Air War, 1914–1918.*

> A British officer is anxious to meet the redoubtable [German] Captain Immelmann in fair fight. The suggested rendezvous is a point above the first line of trenches just east of Hébuterne. The British officer will be there from 10 A.M. to 11 A.M. daily from November 15th till 30th, weather permitting. It is understood that only one aeroplane can be sent to meet this challenge, and that antiaircraft guns may fire at either combatant.

---

the early, heady days of war, when combat appeared glorious and exciting instead of the drudgery it had become. A newspaper correspondent closely watched Ball as he stepped down from his airplane after a mission and got the impression that Ball was ashamed of his role in killing so many Germans.

The specter of death dominated his thoughts more than before. He wrote his father that no pilot who "fought seriously could hope to escape from the war alive,"[34] and when younger brother Cyril considered becoming a pilot, Ball warned him to stay away because the task ruined one's nerves.

On May 7, 1917, Ball accompanied two squadrons in an attack against the home airfield of the famed German ace, Manfred von Richthofen. Although Richthofen was in Germany on leave, his younger brother Lothar led the German response. In a wild melee, opposing pilots paired up and dueled in the skies. One British aviator watched Ball chase a German into a cloud, but no one saw him after that.

His luck had finally run its course. Ball's plane crashed into a farmer's field, where a young French girl rushed out and held the mortally wounded ace in her arms while he died.

In hopes of learning what had happened to their top ace, a few days later the British dropped a note on a German airfield requesting information. On May 18 they officially listed Ball as missing, but no one knew for certain until June 1, when a German note informed the British that Ball had been killed and buried. Lothar von Richthofen claimed he had shot down Ball, but most likely a German machine gunner

German boxers salute the memorial to Albert Ball on the grounds of Nottingham Castle.

shooting from the steeple of a nearby church brought down the British flier.

With a final tally of forty-four kills, Ball's status as hero grew. On June 8, 1917, the British government awarded him the nation's highest military honor, the Victoria Cross, two days before huge crowds attended a grand memorial service at St. Mary's Church in Nottingham. In his honor, a statue of Ball was placed on the grounds of Nottingham castle.

For the duration of the war, surviving Sherwood Foresters remembered their slain comrade. As they headed into battle, they surged forward to the cry, "Remember Captain Ball, Sherwoods!"[35]

Chapter 3

"Ace of Aces"

When people think of World War I flying aces, invariably the names Manfred von Richthofen, Eddie Rickenbacker, and others come to mind. One man who is frequently omitted from that list deserves to be included, for in his career he downed more enemy aircraft—seventy-five—than any flier other than Richthofen. René Fonck, France's "ace of aces," combined incredible flying talent with meticulous preparation to dominate the skies, yet his name is relatively unknown outside of his native France.

An Eager Child

Very little is known of René Fonck's life before World War I. What is known is that Fonck was born on March 27, 1894, in Saulcy-sur-Meurthe, a French town near the Vosges Mountains in eastern France along the Franco-German border. Two influences dominated Fonck's youth—hatred for neighboring Germany and a love of aviation. As a teenager Fonck devoured newspaper and magazine stories depicting the exploits of early French airmen. The feats of stunt pilot Adolphe Pégoud, who in 1913 perfected the death-defying "loop-the-loop" maneuver, and speed racer Roland Garros, who flew 450 miles across the Mediterranean in under eight hours, captivated Fonck. "My instincts had always carried me toward a career in the air," he later wrote in his memoirs. "I had even, one day, without the knowledge of my mother, undergone flight tests."[36]

The other influence gave deadly purpose to Fonck's love of flying. He grew up near the German border and, like most other boys his age, recalled his father's humiliation at France's loss to Germany in the 1870 Franco-Prussian War. A desire for revenge burned in the hearts of most French adults, and as usually occurs, that same revenge sprouted in their offspring. Fonck often mentioned his father's shame in defeat and his own determination to seek vengeance, almost as if he had a duty to redress an old wrong.

When World War I broke out in August 1914 the twenty-year-old Fonck, eager to strike back at the enemy that had so disgraced his father's generation, quickly enlisted in the French army. His first few months proved to be nothing like he had hoped.

Reconnaissance Pilot

Fonck spent his initial five months with the Eleventh Regiment of Engineers, unexciting work that bored the adventurous man. Digging trenches and constructing bridges paled in comparison to combat in the skies, so Fonck requested a transfer to the French Air Arm.

He received his wish early the next year, and in February 1915 he reported for training at the illustrious French military school, St. Cyr. After a few months of training, Fonck reported to a reconnaissance and bombing squadron for his first duties.

Instead of flying into battle in a single-seater fighter, Fonck piloted an unarmed two-seater reconnaissance airplane. While the observer in the rear seat spotted enemy locations and movement below, Fonck flew the aircraft and watched for German fighters intent on shooting them down. His first encounter with a German aircraft produced no fighting, since both craft were unarmed. The enemy reconnaissance plane turned away and Fonck, upset that he could not attack, vowed to never again go into the air without a weapon. Until his airplane was fitted with a machine gun in July 1916, Fonck flew with a rifle beside him.

He had a chance to use it on July 2, 1915, when he again flew near a German two-seater. The excited Fonck fired off a few rounds without result, and since the enemy pilot turned away and headed behind his own lines, Fonck boasted to fellow pilots of his first "victory."

Although the main purpose of flying reconnaissance aircraft was to gather information on the enemy for headquarters, Fonck's

Relatively unknown outside of France, René Fonck is considered one of the greatest combat pilots of World War I.

aggressive style of flying insured that he saw his share of action, especially after he received a machine gun. In May 1916 he and another French pilot were scouting the Verdun region. Since reconnaissance aircraft often had to fly at lower altitudes to gain a better view of movement below, they made tempting targets for German antiaircraft guns. The two flew directly into a thundering barrage that buffeted Fonck's craft from side to side and damaged the other pilot's plane. His companion's plane went into a steep dive that tore away the wings as it descended to French farmland below.

Curiosity almost killed Fonck, who maneuvered his machine too close to the plummeting aircraft. He later recalled, "Fascinated and sickened by the catastrophe, I strayed into the slipstream of Noel's [the other pilot's] plunging aircraft and spun down myself, recovering only a few hundred feet from the ground. The German gunners must have thought they had accounted for both of us at the same time."[37]

Initial Battle Forays

These missions handed Fonck a taste of excitement, but he most wanted to fly a fighter aircraft where he could joust one-on-one with his foe. He preferred flying now more than in his first year, since he at least had a machine gun, but because his main task was to fly for an observer he could not always pursue German planes in individual combat. On occasion, however, opportunities arose.

On August 6, 1916, two German aircraft attacked Fonck as the Frenchman was in the midst of a photographic mission. He skillfully evaded both planes, then decided to fly around in hopes of finding other German aircraft. Fonck headed in the direction of shellbursts, where he dove to attack two Ger-

Fonck accumulated the most kills of World War I pilots, totaling seventy-five by the end of the war.

man aircraft. The first enemy pilot sped away, but Fonck cut off the second plane's avenue of retreat and moved in to gain a shooting position.

Fonck and the German flew in circles for twenty minutes. Each time the German veered right, Fonck followed close on his tail. If the German descended, so did Fonck. The German employed every maneuver he could think of to shake the French pilot, but nothing worked. "After a while, his machine-gunner ceased firing at us and simply stared, white-faced, as though hypnotized,"[38] recalled Fonck.

The German pilot, outclassed by Fonck's superior flying skills, believed he had no choice but to land his craft and surrender. Fonck followed him to the ground, where he and his observer captured the two opponents. Later, under interrogation, the German pilot claimed, "I couldn't do a thing. My adversary had me under his control all the time. He blocked every maneuver I made, dominating me all the time. He had me completely at his mercy."[39]

Even though Fonck did not engage in actual combat as often as he hoped, the experience he gained in a reconnaissance airplane better prepared him for flying a fighter. He learned the intricacies of the two-seater reconnaissance aircraft and knew the best ways to attack a plane that had both a fixed machine gun mounted in the front and a traversible machine gun mounted in the rear. Many Allied pilots who flew only in single-seater airplanes fell to their deaths because they lacked knowledge of the two-

seater. When the time came for Fonck to be his own man, he took this information into combat.

Fighter in His Own Aircraft

On April 25, 1917, Fonck received the orders for which he had waited—to join a squadron of single-seater fighters. He was placed with a unit of renowned aviators whose daring in the skies had already earned the adulation of French men and women. Called the *Escadrille des Cigognes* [Flotilla of the Storks], the unit had one purpose—to hunt the skies and shoot down as many Germans as possible.

Fonck was ready for this next challenge. To be the most effective flier possible, Fonck reduced the art of flying to a science. He constantly exercised so as to be in top physical condition and thus be more alert in the arduous flying conditions that existed, and he meticulously checked his aircraft to catch any imperfections. He examined each bullet that went into his ammunition belt to reduce the possibility of his gun jamming at a critical moment, one of the leading causes of death for aviators, and he spent hours studying relative speeds of airplanes and angles of attack. Fonck refused to believe, as did many pilots, in good or bad luck. He contended that pilots who were careless in minor details paid the ultimate price. However, pilots who prepared properly had a better chance of survival.

Whenever possible he studied downed enemy aircraft to learn about their capabilities. He absorbed every detail such as their

Skill, Not Luck

René Fonck never tired of telling people how good he was. While this irritated other pilots, the French ace was not exaggerating much. American aviator Charles J. Biddle compared Fonck to two other French aces when he wrote the foreword to the American translation of Fonck's memoirs, *Ace of Aces*.

The proof of Fonck's fantastic skill may be appreciated when it is remembered that [Georges] Guynemer was shot down seven times and twice wounded before he was finally killed, and I have a calling card given me by [Charles] Nungesser after the war on which he listed his decorations and seventeen wounds, while Fonck, in the course of several hundred combats in which he had seventy-five official victories and many more that could not be confirmed, was never even touched by a shot from one of his adversaries. One cannot put this down to luck.

top speeds, their tendencies in steep dives, and where blind spots—areas in which the pilot could not see an approaching airplane—existed. Fonck left little to chance.

The French aviator also believed that the flier who maintained a calm demeanor in crises was the flier who emerged triumphant. He wrote that "to obtain good results, you must know how to control your nerves, how to have absolute self-mastery, and how to think coolly in difficult situations."[40]

Where Fonck excelled over other pilots, however, was in his astounding shooting ability. Some pilots fired wildly in the direction of their enemy, but Fonck hated to waste ammunition. He waited until he thought he had the target properly aligned, then fired a brief burst. Usually that was all he needed to bring down his victim.

What made his talent more incredible was that Fonck had to aim not just a machine gun, but his entire aircraft, in the correct position for firing. The bolted machine gun could not swerve to the left or right, so Fonck had to fly the plane with his feet on the rudder pedals, left hand on the controls, right hand on the stick, and two fingers of the right hand touching the gun triggers attached to the stick. Only when his airplane was pointing directly at the enemy—who was of course bobbing and weaving to evade Fonck—did the French aviator open fire.

Vengence and Reflection

Few, if any, pilots fared better. Most aviators put Fonck in a class of his own when it came to shooting, and he rarely needed more than twelve bullets to knock an enemy from the sky. "I put my bullets into the target as if I placed them there by hand,"[41] Fonck unabashedly boasted.

Fonck was in his element with his Spad XIII single-seater. He, like other great French aviators, preferred to hunt for Germans on his own rather than in a group so he would not be slowed by less proficient aviators. Alone, Fonck was free to scour the heavens and chase after any target. He had to be more careful later in the year when the Germans started sending their large killing squadrons into action, but whenever the opportunity arose, Fonck lifted off alone.

He took more caution in September 1917 when the top French ace, Georges Guynemer, was shot down, supposedly by a German pilot named Wissemann. The German was so elated over his victory that he wrote to his family, "Don't worry about me. Never again will I meet an adversary who is half as dangerous as Guynemer."[42]

He was wrong. Devastated by the loss of Guynemer, Fonck vowed to retaliate. Three weeks later he received his chance when he shot down Wissemann in combat.

As Fonck gained familiarity in the sky and confidence in his skills, his killing spree picked up steam. In October 1917, for instance, he shot down ten German planes in a total of only 13.5 hours of flying. During one encounter, an obviously moved Fonck watched the enemy observer fall from his craft to his death. The German pilot dove so quickly to avoid Fonck that the observer in the rear seat toppled out of the airplane, barely missed smashing into Fonck's airplane, then plunged toward the ground.

An exceptional fighter pilot, René Fonck shot down record numbers of German biplanes like this one.

Another encounter with ground troops left Fonck reflecting on the devastation he and others caused. To smash a German offensive, Fonck received orders to strafe lines of German soldiers that were marching across roadways and fields. The sight of the enemy infantry as he swooped low to machine gun the men did not leave the pilot.

"All day long the air was filled with the roar of engines. We flew so low that we almost touched the enemy's bayonets, watching the compact masses of troops wilt away before our machine-gun fire. The chaos was terrible. Panic-stricken horses charged in all directions, trampling soldiers underneath."[43]

"A Tiresome Braggart"

Most pilots possess a strong personality that borders on cockiness. Only by assuming that one has the talent to fly against the best does one have a chance of surviving, so most top fliers acted with an infectious sense of assuredness.

Fonck was no different in having that attitude, but he added to it a sense of self-importance that others lacked. He believed that he was better than the rest, and did things to underline those differences. While other aviators smelled of gasoline or walked about with grease smudges on their uniforms, the handsome man with a pencil-thin mustache wore nothing but cleaned and pressed clothes. Other men in the squadron kept pets, such as cats and dogs, but Fonck purchased a stork. Instead of joining the rest for wine and song, Fonck took long naps or worked on his bodybuilding.

Although Fonck served his country well, his fellow aviators tired of his arrogance and obsession with image.

What most irritated his fellow pilots, though, was Fonck's continual tendency to brag about his accomplishments, which were considerable enough on their own. If a pilot returned from a mission to relate an adventure, Fonck later landed with a more incredible tale. He claimed that one time a loose fuel connection forced him down deep inside German territory, where he hastily repaired the faulty mechanism and took off before rushing enemy soldiers arrived. He stated that he was clearly the best shot among French pilots, and loved to claim that no German bullet ever touched his aircraft.

One time he and two other pilots returned from a furious dogfight in which German and French planes freely mingled and shot at each other. A German had been shot down, and all three Frenchmen claimed the downed aircraft as theirs. The other two pilots agreed to cut a deck of cards to determine who should receive credit, but Fonck refused to go along. He insisted that his bullets had downed the enemy aircraft and that he should be able to record the victory as his. His two compatriots, undoubtedly miffed at Fonck's intransigence, reluctantly gave in and allowed Fonck to take credit.

"He is not a truthful man," declared one of Fonck's few close friends, French ace Claude Haegelen. "He is a tiresome braggart, and even a bore, but in the air a slashing rapier, a steel blade tempered with unblemished courage and priceless skill. But afterwards he can't forget how he rescued you, nor let you forget it. He can almost make you wish he hadn't helped you in the first place."[44]

The Master Battler

The man might have been overindulgent with self-praise, but he could back up his statements with action. On March 15, 1918, he spotted a German reconnaissance plane a thousand yards below him. The German, busy photographing French troop emplace-

ments, failed to notice Fonck as the pilot swooped in for the kill.

"I was twenty meters away, and neither the observer nor the pilot had budged yet. It would have been easy for me to shoot them down without giving them a chance to know what hit them." Rather than attack an unaware enemy, Fonck decided to wait until they saw him. Finally the observer turned "and our looks, like two crossed swords, were exchanged. He bolted up from his cockpit like a jack-in-the-box. Panic-stricken, he touched the shoulder of his comrade to call his attention to my approach, and the pilot visibly experienced a rapid shudder." Before the German could bring his machine gun around, Fonck fired. "From my

Death Stalks the Table

A young man entered the field of aviation knowing that, in wartime, his chances of survival were not very good. The thrill of lifting to the skies, however, offset the specter that only months or years remained in their brief lives. René Fonck lived for years after the war, but the feeling lingered among members of his squadron that time, rather than being an ally, was a foe. One of Fonck's fellow pilots starkly emphasized that fact with a comment he made during one dinner when he noticed that thirteen men had gathered to dine. The remark is taken from Thomas R. Funderburk's *The Fighters: The Men and Machines of the First Air War.*

> For the Chinese, thirteen at the table means that one of the number will die within the year. For us, however, this can have little significance since a year from now certainly more than one of us is going to be dead.

Vickers [machine gun], in rapid succession, little sparks, similar to Morse code signals, burst out in staccato fashion; and while the enemy observer collapsed over the fuselage, the Albatros, dealt a death blow, went down in a tailspin crashing on the earth below."[45]

Two months later, on May 9, Fonck recorded one of the most amazing deeds of his career when he shot down six German aircraft in one day. He notched the first three in under one minute, landed for more fuel and ammunition, than rose again to shoot down three more aircraft in less than six minutes. With only fifty-two total bullets used—an average of less than nine per plane—Fonck destroyed six German airplanes in seven minutes.

Veteran aviators point to his August 1918 mission as proof of his deadly accuracy. He attacked three German aircraft and shot them all down so quickly that they crash-landed in the same French field less than one hundred yards apart.

After Fonck shot down another eleven aircraft in ten days, he headed to the hospital to visit the sole German pilot to survive, a German ace named Lieutenant Wusthoff who had recorded twenty-seven kills. During his chat with Fonck, Wusthoff remarked that he and the other German pilots knew little of Fonck's tactics. The Frenchman looked at him, then replied, "That's not surprising. My opponents don't usually survive to talk about me."[46]

Fonck recorded his final kill only ten days before the war ended. A German propaganda aircraft was dropping leaflets stat-ing that the Allies had lost the war when Fonck's bullets knocked it from the sky. The plane became his seventy-fifth official victory, even though Fonck claimed to have shot down 127. He argued that since most of his fighting occurred over German lines, his victims often crashed in German-held territory and thus could not be verified. More amazing than his total, though, was that in a war in which few top aces survived, Fonck was never wounded in battle and his airplane never suffered serious damage. Be-

On May 8, 1918, Fonck was awarded the Legion d'Honneur.

Between the world wars, Fonck developed a friendship with German pilot Hermann Goering (seated in cockpit).

cause of this, some historians and aviation specialists claim that Fonck, and not the immortal Red Baron from Germany, was the foremost ace of World War I.

After the War

Sadly, Fonck's postwar world did not end as happily as his service days. He entered civil aviation and became an expert in aerobatics and demonstration flying, appearing at air shows around Europe with his name boldly emblazoned in huge letters across the plane's fuselage. Drawn by the attractive financial rewards, he tried to organize an attempt to become the first pilot to navigate the Atlantic Ocean. He traveled to New York, where on September 21, 1926, he taxied down the runway to take off for Europe, but the overburdened aircraft, heavily weighed down with gasoline, failed to become airborne. The craft overran the airstrip and burst into flames.

Fonck and his supporters ordered a replacement craft and prepared for a second attempt, but before they had another

"That's the Way It Was"

In the latter eighteen months of the war, pilots engaged in massive aerial battles called dogfights. Instead of locking onto an opposing aircraft and following it to an end, men most often simply shot at whatever target entered their field of vision. American aviator George Vaughn describes his typical encounter, as quoted in Arthur Gordon's *The American Heritage History of Flight*.

> Most people seem to think a dogfight is just two airplanes going round and round and round for minutes and minutes at a time until one shoots the other down. As a rule, it didn't work out that way because there were so many in the sky that you jumped from one to the other, and two or three of them shot at you, not just one. You shot at four or five—anybody you could get your sights on—and then another one. It was usually just two or three bursts [of fire], and then maybe you were on another fellow or maybe somebody was on you by this time. That's the way it was.

opportunity, Charles A. Lindbergh made his historic flight and Fonck moved on to other matters.

One of the numerous contacts Fonck made in the aviation field happened to be a German fighter pilot from the war. In the spring of 1920, while Fonck was on business in Sweden, a German pilot there contacted him and asked his help in landing a job in the aviation field. Work was then scarce in postwar Germany, gripped in the throes of an agonizing economic depression, so Fonck readily agreed to help a fellow warrior. He contacted a few people, and before long Hermann Goering, who would later rise to head Adolf Hitler's air force, found work.

The move returned to torment Fonck, who remained in touch with Goering. In 1940, after Germany overran and occupied much of France in World War II, French leaders asked Fonck to use his ties with Goering to determine what Hitler intended to do with France. Fonck agreed and subsequently visited Goering several times over two years.

Following the war, many French leaders stood trial for collaborating with the Germans. Although Fonck was not among the accused, his name came up during the trials. Fonck's friendship with Goering tarnished the French pilot's reputation, and the onetime war hero lived the remainder of his life under a cloud of suspicion.

Fonck retired from a government inspection post in 1939. He lived in Paris until his death on June 18, 1953, at the age of fifty-nine.

Chapter 4

Death on a Picket Fence

E ach aviator in this volume could be described as a unique individual. Only one, however, flew in the war for two different nations. After serving in the French Air Arm for the first two years, he joined a special unit composed entirely of American pilots, even though the United States was not officially at war. With that country's entry in the spring of 1917, the aviator became part of a famous American squadron that included other noted fliers. Raoul Lufbery, the man from two nations, left his imprint wherever he flew.

French-American Influences

Raoul Lufbery was born in Clermont, France, on March 14, 1885, to an American father and French mother. One year later, following the unfortunate death of his mother, Lufbery was placed in the care of relatives while his father headed out into the world to establish his business and pursue his hobby of collecting stamps. In 1890, Lufbery's father remarried, and the next

year the entire family traveled to the United States and settled in Wallingford, Connecticut.

Though father and son lived together for a time, they did not develop a strong bond. Lufbery spent the formative years of his life in France with other members of the Lufbery clan, and his father placed more devotion to his growing stamp collection than he did to his son. In 1901, when Lufbery's stepmother died, the youth again lacked any strong parental influence.

After working in a chocolate factory for three years, Lufbery, now an American citizen, joined the U.S. Army in 1908. He served for two years in the Philippines and recorded top honors for marksmanship, placing first in his regiment in that skill.

When his two years ended in 1910, Lufbery drifted through the Far East seeking adventure. He bounced around China and India, seeing all the exotic spots those nations offered, then supported himself by working at a variety of jobs—as a server in top restaurants, unloading boats, working on ships steaming between Europe and Africa, and even racing cars. Although he lived from day to day, Lufbery always managed to earn enough money to survive.

In one of his wanderings through the Far East, Lufbery encountered a French pilot named Marc Pourpe, an adventurer who traveled the world giving flying demonstrations and taking passengers into the air for a price. The airplane fascinated Lufbery, who became a close friend to Pourpe as well as his mechanic. For two years the friends

Raoul Lufbery served two nations during World War I, France and the United States.

toured Asia and Africa, thrilling crowds with their aerial exhibitions. In 1914, Pourpe set a record by flying nonstop from Cairo, Egypt, to Khartoum in Sudan, a distance of eleven hundred miles.

Later that summer the two headed to France, where they intended to purchase a new airplane for further travels around the world. Before they could embark on another overseas trip, however, events embroiled Europe in World War I.

Escadrille Lafayette

Along with thousands of other French citizens, the pair attempted to enlist in the French military. Pourpe was accepted into the French Air Arm, but to Lufbery's disappointment, the French declined his application because he was an American citizen.

Not to be thwarted in his goal of flying with Pourpe, Lufbery joined the French foreign legion, a military outfit that accepted men from anywhere in the world. Service with the foreign legion automatically entitled a man to claim the benefits of French citizenship, and as soon as he could, Lufbery applied for a transfer to Pourpe's unit as his mechanic.

Lufbery's ploy worked, and the two good friends were reunited in late 1914. Sadly, the pair had little time to enjoy their duties as Pourpe was shot down and killed on December 2. Lufbery vowed to avenge his friend's death and entered pilot training. After six months of training, during which the novice flier crashed so many airplanes that instructors almost tossed him

out of the program, Lufbery received his wings in July 1915. He hoped to be placed in a fighter squadron, but his superiors, recalling the aircraft he had damaged in training, posted Lufbery to a bomber unit.

Lufbery remained with the bombing squadron for the rest of 1915. Determined to get into a fighter unit, however, Lufbery practiced flying in a single-seater aircraft as often as possible.

While Lufbery labored to perfect his flying skills, another American organized the air unit in which Lufbery first gained fame. Edmund Gros, an American physician who resided in Paris, wanted to gather every American fighting for the French into one aviation unit. In the fall of 1915 he asked the French government for permission to inter-

Before joining the French Air arm, Lufbery enlisted in the French foreign legion to attain French citizenship.

view Americans serving in the French army, then spent the rest of the year searching the foreign legion, the infantry, and other military arms for volunteers. When Gros found willing individuals, he used his connections with top French officials to arrange a transfer to the French Air Arm for training. By April 1916, Gros had gathered enough men, including some volunteers who traveled across the Atlantic, to form the *Escadrille Americaine*. Lufbery, excited to be flying with a fighter squadron, was one of the first to join.

"Contact!"

Lifting off from the runway in World War I entailed an entirely different set of actions than today's modern planes require. Since he flew in an open cockpit, the pilot first put on a fur-lined, fur-collared flying suit and a fur-lined leather helmet for protection from the biting cold. While he prepared, the crew walked the aircraft out of the hangar to the field, then placed blocks underneath the wheels to prevent the plane from moving. Once the pilot hopped into the machine, a mechanic turned the propeller over a few times by hand with the ignition off so that oil and gasoline would gush into the cylinders. Then at the mechanic's yell of "Contact!" the pilot turned on the switch. The man at the propeller gave the blade a sharp downward jerk, then quickly stepped back to avoid losing an arm or hand to the whirling blade. Carefully the pilot increased power to the engine and taxied down the runway for a liftoff.

The unit quickly proved its worth. From April until September 1916 they shot down seventeen German aircraft in the Verdun region before being transferred to the Somme, where they participated in the heavy air combat occurring every day above the killing fields below. With the American symbol of an Indian head painted on the aircrafts' fuselages, the Americans charged into battle with such effectiveness that the German government protested that the use of the word *Americaine* violated U.S. neutrality. On December 6, 1916, the French government bowed to American pressure and changed the name to the *Escadrille Lafayette* after the French officer who assisted the colonists in the American Revolution.

A Natural

Lufbery joined the unit on May 24, 1916. For one of the few times in his life, Lufbery fit in with the rest, for they consisted of adventurers and seekers of excitement just like him. Sons of wealthy business magnates rubbed elbows with soldiers of fortune and ordinary sailors. Lufbery, who had never forged familial bonds, enjoyed the companionship of his fellow pilots.

His first month proved to be the opposite of what he expected, as the men flew in a fairly quiet sector. One of the pilots remembered the sumptuous meals they enjoyed, where they ate "delicious trout from a neighboring stream, fat chickens, game, hares, wild-fowl, carefully cooked and washed down with generous burgundy."[47]

The peacefulness quickly dissipated. Lufbery recorded his first kill on July 30, 1916, when he shot down a German airplane as he returned from a routine patrol. The next week he added two more kills to his total, and on October 12, when he shot down his fifth aircraft in a large raid against a German ammunition factory, Lufbery became the first American ace of the war.

Fellow pilots claimed that Lufbery was a natural flier as well as a gifted mechanic. When he flew, it appeared that he and the machine melded as one unit, that the wings were simply extensions of Lufbery's arms and the engine an addition to his brain. Lufbery became so skilled at performing stunts that he frequently entertained the unit after they returned from missions. His severe loops and spins strained the capabilities of his airplane but astonished the men on the ground.

He trusted his machine because he knew how every part functioned. With his background of repairing engines for Pourpe, he excelled at getting the most out of his aircraft and developed such a stellar reputation that a fellow aviator claimed, "Lufbery was a wonderful mechanic and his plane was always the best in the *Escadrille.* Anyone would rather have a second-hand Lufbery machine than a new one, anytime."[48]

Lufbery succeeded in the air because he exercised caution at every opportunity. He preferred to attack either from below or at odd angles so that the enemy gunner could not shoot at him, and he tried to avoid approaching the rear gunners, which everyone considered the most dangerous German guns in use. Lufbery also loved to circle at higher altitudes with the sun at his back, then swoop on unsuspecting enemy planes. If he were attacked, Lufbery allowed the pursuer to close the distance, then embarked on an intricate loop to flip positions and settle on his opponent's tail. Should that or other maneuvers fail, Lufbery swayed from side to side to make it harder for the German gunner to hit his target.

On May 24, 1916, Lufbery (bottom, fourth from left), joined the Escadrille Lafayette, *serving as a pilot and as a mechanic.*

He usually evaded his foe, but Lufbery had his share of close calls. On December 27, 1916, he returned to base with several bullet holes gracing his airplane. When he stepped out of the cockpit, he noticed that one bullet had even passed through his flight jacket.

A Public Hero

Both France and Great Britain honored Lufbery's accomplishments. The French awarded him the distinguished Croix de Guerre, while the British made him the first American ever to receive the Military Cross. Adulation grew in both France, the land of his birth, and the United States, his adoptive country. Women followed him as he walked about town, husbands and wives named children after him, French chefs created dishes in his honor, and mail poured in from both North America and Europe.

American pilots could walk into bars crowded by French aces, but it was Lufbery who received the attention. "How we unheroic and unknown airmen envied him the greetings he had from such men as [Georges] Guynemer, [René] Fonck, [Charles] Nungesser and others who had achieved greatly,"[49] said James Norman Hall, fellow pilot who later coauthored the famous *Mutiny on the Bounty*.

Despite the notoriety, the quiet Lufbery remained unchanged. Instead of stating that his skill and talent resulted in victories, he credited simple luck for his achievements. Hall explained that Lufbery

never boasted or took credit himself. He counted his success as three-fourths luck, and was always surprised that so much of it should come his way. When foolish people tried to flatter him, he used to say to us after they had gone, "Well, you know, it's funny what things people will say to a man's face. I wonder if they think we like it?" He had to take a lot of it whether he liked it or not.[50]

On occasion, Lufbery exhibited a devilish streak. For example, he and two other fliers purchased a lion cub in Paris, named him Whiskey after their escapades in French bars, and kept him as a squadron pet. Another time he and fellow pilot, Bert Hall, headed into Paris for a night on the town. They met a group of beautiful young females, invited them to dinner, then enjoyed a grand feast in an exquisite restaurant. Hall became so absorbed chatting with the girls that he failed to notice that Lufbery had carefully sneaked away and left him with the bill.

Normally, though, Lufbery preferred calmer activities. He spent more time alone than most of the others, who had parents and loved ones to write to, and went for long walks in the woods. He often returned with an armful of wild mushrooms for everyone to enjoy in the mess hall.

The *Escadrille Lafayette* continued in operation until the United States entered the war in April 1917. Lufbery and the others, who had recorded fifty-seven downed German aircraft compared to the loss of nine

Lufbery became a celebrated hero in France, Britain, and the United States, receiving the French Croix de Guerre and the British Military Cross.

American pilots, had to wait until the American military was organized for battle before being transferred to a unit in the U.S. Air Service. After seven long months, on November 7, 1917, the *Escadrille Lafayette* officially became part of the U.S. armed forces.

"To Be in His Company Was an Honor"

Lufbery remained with the *Escadrille Lafayette* until January 5, 1918, when he was sent to an administrative duty. Chafing to return to the skies, Lufbery instead spent most of January as a clerk while he waited for a squadron posting. He hated the time away from the front, where he knew his ample flying skills could contribute far more to the war effort than shuffling papers behind a desk in some office far from the fighting.

He quickly tired of the tediousness and boredom, sometimes snapping sarcastically to others. For instance, one day a commanding officer lined up all the men to explain the importance of maintaining healthy teeth. He illustrated how to properly brush up and down rather than sideways, made the men promise to take care of their

55

teeth, then handed each soldier a toothbrush. An incredulous Lufbery turned to the man standing next to him and remarked, "I wonder if he thinks the boys are going to bite the Germans."[51]

In February, Lufbery finally received orders to join the Ninety-Fifth Aero Squadron, the first aviation unit of the American military in Europe. Since the United States wanted experienced combat pilots in charge of the new units, in early April, Lufbery was made commanding officer of the companion group, the Ninety-fourth Aero Pursuit Squadron, and told to train the new fliers in the art of aerial warfare.

Lufbery proved to be a master teacher. He instructed his new charges, which included a young aviator named Eddie Rickenbacker, to approach the enemy with extreme caution, to attack when the odds were favorable, and to always remain calm under fire. He emphasized that panic produced death, and that the best way to avoid panic was to be totally familiar with both their own machines and those of the Germans, and to practice as much as possible. When a young pilot asked what to do if an enemy bullet caused a fire to break out in the airplane, Lufbery explained how to angle the aircraft so the flames would blow away from the pilot while he descended with all due haste.

Rickenbacker claimed that Lufbery's most valuable advice concerned how to spot the Germans before being seen by them. Lufbery explained that many pilots made the mistake of staring at one location for too

Lufbery Meets Rickenbacker

Eddie Rickenbacker's exploits gained him the distinction of being the greatest American ace of the war. He never tired, however, of giving credit to the man who preceded him into combat and laid the foundation for American aviators. In his memoirs, *Rickenbacker,* he describes his hero, with whom he served in the Ninety-forth Aero Pursuit Squadron.

> Even more impressive was the presence of the greatest pilot of them all, Major Raoul Lufbery, the American Ace of Aces. He had shot down seventeen enemy aircraft. Lufbery, a native of France, had emigrated to the United States as a young man but had returned to fight for his native land. He was the idol of two countries.

long. Instead, he urged his pilots to scan the skies with a side movement of the head. "In my conversations with Lufbery, he had described a kind of corkscrew maneuver that he used when flying near the lines," mentioned Rickenbacker, who later became the leading American ace of the war. "Flying in this manner, turning the head rhythmically from side to side, the pilot could sweep the skies with his eyes, checking everything above and below, to the right and to the left. I tried to follow his corkscrew path through the skies, but it did not come easily."[52]

Lufbery the Teacher

Rickenbacker and the other American pilots treated Lufbery as an icon. His exploits had been recorded in American newspapers, and Lufbery's name was legend in the military, so pilots considered it the ultimate compliment to be placed in Lufbery's unit. "Simply to be in his company was an honor," said Rickenbacker, "but of more practical value was his knowledge of air combat. He was a quiet individual with a dry sense of humor, and he recognized my eagerness to learn."[53]

The two fliers spent hours discussing combat and aerial maneuvers. Lufbery, who had never had much of a family let alone a little brother, came to see Rickenbacker as someone who looked up to him and as an individual Lufbery could help. The newly arrived American showed prowess with an airplane, and Lufbery was impressed with Rickenbacker's dedication to being the best pilot. The youngster seemed to absorb Lufbery's every word. Rickenbacker, who forged a close bond with Lufbery, explained that "if he felt that you had the qualities and the interest in becoming a real fighter pilot he would go out of his way to give you the benefit of his knowledge."[54]

One example of his generous teaching style occurred on March 6, 1918. After holding what amounted to classroom discussion for a few weeks, Lufbery announced that he would take two pilots over German lines for the unit's first mission. Each man hoped to be one of the two selected; Lufbery settled on Rickenbacker and another pilot named Douglas Campbell.

The trio lifted off and headed toward enemy lines. They flew around for a while, then returned to base from an uneventful flight. When the three landed, Lufbery remained in the background while the excited Rickenbacker and Campbell shared details of the mission with the other pilots. When asked if they had seen any airplanes, both young aviators replied in the negative.

"Sure there weren't any other planes around, Rick?" asked Lufbery. "Not a one!" replied Rickenbacker.

Lufbery shook his head in amusement, then mentioned the fifteen aircraft he spotted.

> One formation of five Spads [a type of aircraft] crossed under us before we passed the lines. Another flight of five Spads went by about fifteen minutes later, five hundred yards away. Damn good things they weren't the Boches [Germans]. And there were four German Albatroses ahead of us when we turned back and another enemy two-seater closer to us than that. You must learn to look around.[55]

Lufbery grinned, then took the men to Rickenbacker's plane and pointed to the bullet holes in the fabric. For the entire mission Rickenbacker, who possessed an abundance of talent, was unaware of the enemy and of how close the bullets had come to hitting him.

In one of their quiet chats, Lufbery mentioned that he preferred flying on his own to his new task of leading other men into battle. He missed the freedom to search for Germans as a solitary hunter, but realized that he had a duty to perform for his nation. "There's a hell of a lot of difference in going out alone, no matter what the odds are against you, and in going out as a member or a leader of a group of pilots who may or may not be as good as you are," Lufbery mentioned. "It's a great responsibility to shepherd these pilots out and get back home safe. I prefer to fight alone, on my own."[56]

The only item holding back Lufbery's new charges was that for the first month or so they had to fly unarmed airplanes. Incredibly, the men and planes had been sent across the Atlantic but the machine guns had not yet arrived. Lufbery thus had to take extra precautions to ensure that he did not lead his raw aviators into situations they could not easily escape.

The lack of armament angered the veteran. He exploded to James Norman Hall,

"It's nearly a year since the United States declared war, and what do you suppose the 94th is doing? Waiting for machine guns! Six hundred million dollars is appropriated for the United States Air Service, and we're loafing. We can't get enough guns to equip a dozen planes!"[57]

Finally, on April 10, 1918, the guns arrived. Mechanics quickly mounted the weapons to the aircraft, and within hours the Americans headed to the skies in search of their quarry. On April 18 the Ninety-Fourth Aero Squadron recorded its first two kills when Alan Winslow and Douglas Campbell each shot down a German aircraft.

Death of A Hero

Throughout this first month, Lufbery continued to lead his squadron in missions and, as always, discussed the flights with his men afterward. During one chat with Rickenbacker, Lufbery talked about the one aspect of flying that most pilots either avoided thinking about or hated to consider. What would a man do if he were trapped five thousand feet above the ground in a burning airplane—remain with the craft and face painful death by fire, or jump quickly to certain death? Since upper-echelon military commanders believed that parachutes induced a pilot to leave his aircraft before he should, parachutes had not come into popular use. Thus leaping provided nothing more than a less gruesome way to die.

Lufbery had no doubts about his selection. "I'd stay with the machine," he mentioned to his student. "If you jump you

Watch for the Enemy

American pilot Douglas Campbell, the first American flier to shoot down a German aircraft, quickly learned the importance of having superb eyesight in the skies. Two men whose exploits in the air became legendary—Raoul Lufbery and Eddie Rickenbacker—accompanied Campbell on his initial mission over German lines. Author Arthur Gordon included the following account in his *The American Heritage History of Flight*, in which Campbell recalled the lessons he absorbed from his cohorts.

We flew around for about an hour and a half while the gasoline would last, and it all seemed very dull. When we got back Lufbery asked us what we saw, and we hadn't seen anything—but he'd seen a couple of German planes not very far away. The secret of seeing them was not to focus—just gaze around. Then anything that crossed your field of vision you'd see.

In April 1918, Lufbery (right) became commanding officer of the Ninety-Fourth Aero Pursuit Squadron, where he trained new fliers.

haven't got a chance. If you stay, you may be able to side-slip your plane down so that you can fan the flames away from yourself. Perhaps you can even put the fire out before you reach the ground."[58]

The conversation proved to be a harbinger of the future. On May 19, as Lufbery relaxed in his barracks, a German observation plane approached the American airfield. Lufbery ran outside, jumped on a motorcycle, and raced to the airfield. Since mechanics were working on his airplane, Lufbery hopped in another plane and took off in pursuit of the German.

At two thousand feet Lufbery attacked. He fired several bursts at the observation plane before pulling out of the dive, then plunged in a second charge. This time his guns jammed, and Lufbery had to divert his attention from the German to his own weapon. Soldiers watching from the ground could see Lufbery pounding on the gun to free the stuck bullets, which he soon dislodged, but before he could continue his attack the German machine gunner riddled Lufbery's plane.

Lufbery died tragically on May 19, 1918, when the guns of his aircraft jammed.

Observers watched in horror as Lufbery tried to steady his damaged aircraft. He kept the plane heading in a straight direction for a few seconds before flames engulfed the cockpit. Lufbery crawled out of his seat and straddled the fuselage in an attempt to shuffle away from the flames and toward the tail, but the inferno quickly overtook him. He sat still for a few more seconds, facing the horrendous choice he had discussed with Rickenbacker, then jumped over the side of the blazing airplane.

Rickenbacker and a group of pilots piled into a car and headed to the spot where Lufbery's body had hit the ground. "He had fallen in a lovely little garden in a small town near Nancy," wrote Rickenbacker. "Nearby was a small stream; he may have been trying to land in the water. Instead his body had been impaled on a picket fence. Death must have been instantaneous."[59]

Lufbery's demise angered his fellow pilots, who argued that a parachute could have saved his life. Their pleas came too late for Lufbery, however. The man who flew for two nations, who trained inexperienced American aviators in the art of aerial combat and gave so much valuable knowledge to others, lay shattered on the same French soil on which he had been born.

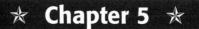

Chapter 5

"No Hun Will Ever Shoot Down Mick"

Most World War I aces endangered their lives so frequently by jumping into their unreliable aircraft because they possessed a deep passion for both flying and working with machines. They shot at and tried to kill the enemy almost as an afterthought—feeling the wind in their face and trodding a domain once exclusively belonging to the clouds propelled them to greater efforts. England's Mick Mannock, however, possessed different demons. His desire was specific: He wanted to hunt down and kill Germans.

Dysfunctional Family Life

Edward "Mick" Mannock was born on May 24, 1887, in Aldershot, an English army training ground. His father, a Scotsman who served in the British army, took little interest in his growing family of five children and an English wife, and since corporals in the military earned paltry wages, Mannock's mother had to work instead of remaining at home and raising the children. As a result Mannock and his siblings often lacked parental supervision and attention.

Conditions worsened in 1899 when Mannock's father abandoned the family after his military service expired. The twelve-year-old Mannock and his brother dropped out of school to help their mother support the family. The youth, who suffered from poor eyesight in his left eye because of an illness, worked first in a grocery store, where he swept floors and carried heavy bags of produce, then in a barber shop, where he lathered the customers' chins and picked up trash.

Although the family struggled financially, Mannock's mother steadfastly believed that she and her children could survive on their own efforts. She disdained charity as nothing more than a handout to weak people. One time Mannock came home with a pile of secondhand clothes given to him by a friend's parents. Mannock's mother was so upset that she stuffed the clothes behind the kitchen stove so her children would not wear them.

Edward "Mick" Mannock's disdain for the Germans motivated him to become a fighter pilot.

Mannock gained a surrogate father when he landed a job climbing telephone poles for the National Telephone Company out of Canterbury, England. Since the posting (job location) was too far from home, young Mannock roomed with James Eyles and his wife, a childless couple who shared love and tenderness with the youth. For the remainder of his life Mannock treated the Eyles as parents.

At the end of 1913, Mannock traveled to Turkey as an inspector for lines installed by his telephone company. War erupted while Mannock worked in that nation, and when Turkey sided with Germany, Mannock joined hundreds of other British citizens in Turkish detention camps. He remained in camp until April 1915, when Turkish officials sent him back to England. They figured that a twenty-seven-year-old man with poor eyesight, also suffering from severe dysentery (an disease of the intestines) due to his confinement, could hardly be a threat to them or Germany in the war. This assessment proved to be dismally incorrect.

To the Front

Mannock joined a medical unit upon his return to England and after recovering from the dysentery. Eager for more action than treating the wounded, Mannock transferred to the Royal Engineers, where he faced the prospect of planting explosives in tunnels dug underneath the German positions. In words that chillingly exemplified his hatred for the enemy, he wrote home, "I'm going to be a tunneling officer and blow the bastards up. The higher they go and the more pieces that come down, the better!"[60]

Even this proved too passive for Mannock, who next requested a transfer to the Royal Flying Corps. His commanding officer attempted to dissuade Mannock, claiming that airplanes were nothing more than death traps, but the determined Mannock was not to be swayed. Even though he suffered from poor eyesight in his left eye, Mannock faked his way through the eye examination—probably by memorizing the eye chart—passed flight training in November 1916, and received orders to report to No. 40 Squadron in France in April 1917.

Mannock arrived at the front during an abysmal period for the English. The Germans so dominated the skies—they shot down forty-four British aircraft on April 6 alone—that the month became known to British fliers as "Bloody April." Mannock compounded the situation on his first day by walking into the unit mess hall and sitting in an empty chair, an action that produced angry stares and embarrassing silence among the other pilots. Mannock later learned that the chair was the one normally used by a pilot who had been shot down and killed that day.

He also did not endear himself to fellow aviators when he appeared hesitant to enter battle during his first few days of flying. The men had no way of knowing about Mannock's poor vision in one eye, and the newcomer had simply been practicing and learning all he could to compensate for the

World War I fighter planes had no radios. Pilots were dependent on Royal engineers (pictured) to maintain forward position land lines.

deficiency. He spent hours learning how to maneuver his craft and figuring out the best way to accurately fire his machine gun with one good eye. When a handful of members wondered about Mannock's courage the squadron commander, Capt. G. L. Lloyd, told them to give him time. Lloyd added that when Mannock was ready, he would quickly assert his skill.

He almost never made it to combat. On April 19, Mannock flew at two thousand feet when a portion of his aircraft's wing broke off and fell away. Normally that meant death for the pilot, but somehow Mannock regained enough control of the airplane to land safely. He later recalled, "Such a thing

Hazards in a Balloon

Observation balloons yielded significant information about the enemy, but they also placed the man in the balloon in considerable danger. Artillery shells zoomed his way from opposing trenches, and aircraft attacked almost every day. To give protection to balloonists, in 1915 the French provided them with parachutes. The device did not always work as intended, as explained in the following excerpt from Lee Kennett's *The First Air War, 1914–1918.*

> It was not as good a solution as it might seem, for the parachutes of the day were not wholly reliable, and though the parachute was suspended for instant use and the observer was already harnessed to it, it was hard for him to evacuate the basket cleanly and quickly with 20,000 cubic feet of hydrogen igniting over his head. The parachute fouled all too frequently; or it might open cleanly, only to have the burning mass of the balloon fall on it.

has never happened before where the pilot has not been killed or injured by the fall."[61]

By May 7, Mannock felt confident enough to engage the enemy, and within a few weeks he proved Captain Lloyd's words to be prophetic. He shot down an observation balloon on May 7, added a German two-seater on June 7, then added four more by mid-July.

He experienced the first of his close brushes with death in combat on May 9 when three German aircraft pounced on him. Mannock tried to return fire but his guns jammed. When the engine quit, Mannock felt he had little chance of survival, but he veered his craft downward from sixteen thousand feet and zigzagged to avoid the stream of bullets. At 3,000 feet the engine suddenly kicked back to life, and Mannock hastened away. "I turned away and landed here with my knees shaking and my nerves all torn to bits," he confided to his diary. "I feel a bit better now, but all my courage seems to have gone after that experience this morning."[62]

Like other successful pilots, Mannock learned something each time he went into the sky. He realized that if his airplane were hit over enemy territory and he had to land, he should try to descend as far from the trenches as possible. Troops stationed to the rear were far more likely to treat airmen with kindness than infantrymen who endured the horrors of the trenches.

His exploits gained Mannock a Military Cross, promotion to captain, and status as flight commander on July 22, 1917. In that capacity Mannock showed great prowess at passing along his knowledge to less experienced pilots. He taught his men how to perform aerobatics to increase their confidence in flying, but emphasized that in battle one must rely only on sharp turns to evade the enemy. He constantly repeated what he termed his golden rule about the approach for any attack—"Always above [the enemy aircraft], seldom on the same level, never beneath."[63]

Some moments called for daring above and beyond his advice. On September 5, 1917, Mannock noticed that another aircraft had been following him. Unable to determine whether it was friend or foe, Mannock slowed down and allowed the aircraft to inch closer. He believed that if the craft were English, the pilot would simply fly on without firing, but if it were German, the nose would dip, indicating an attack. Mannock waited until he saw the pursuing aircraft dip down, then quickly spun his airplane around, dove down, and came up directly behind the stunned German. A few rounds sent the enemy machine to the field below.

No. 74 Squadron

At the end of 1917, Mannock received orders to report as commanding officer of No. 74 Squadron, the unit with which he forged the closest ties. Mannock shepherded his men like they were his own family, imparting whatever wisdom he had accumulated in his brief time at the front and making sure they were prepared for battle.

One of the newer pilots, Lt. Ira Jones, quickly overcame his apprehension after first meeting with Mannock.

I arrived at the Squadron late at night, rather shy and frightened. Mannock was in the Mess, and he looked after me just like a big brother. I was posted to his Flight, and he did not allow me to cross the lines for over a week; during this time he took me up twice on a line patrol and we had several practice flights. His advice to me was always to follow my leader, keep my eyes and ears open and keep a silent tongue. It was wonderful to be in his Flight; to him his Flight was everything and he lived for it. Every member had his special thought and care.[64]

On another occasion Mannock noticed a fresh arrival who kept to himself rather than join the other men at the dining table. Mannock sensed the boy's fear, and when he learned that the youth had lied about his age and was only seventeen, Mannock persuaded his commanding officer to hold the newcomer out of battle for a week.

In that time Mannock took him under his wing and taught him how to be a proficient combat pilot. When Mannock felt the pilot was ready, he told the young man that it was time to get his first German, and the pair headed across the lines into enemy territory. The British youngster notched his first kill, but he handed the honor to Mannock, who had all but placed the German aircraft in the youth's gunsights.

It was really Captain Mannock who did it all. It was after his patrol and he took me

Mannock's Combat Reports

Mick Mannock gained almost as much attention for his brief combat reports as for his astounding battle engagements. In his book *Fighter Pilots of World War I*, Robert Jackson includes the report filed by Mannock on June 1, 1918, which shows his preference to avoid boosting his own image.

> Observed and engaged formation of EA scouts [German aircraft] east of Merville. Attacked from the front and above. The highest Scout being behind, SE [Mannock's plane] opened fire with both guns at point-blank range. The EA's bottom wings fell off and it crashed.
>
> Engaged another EA and after a short vertical burst at close range, this Scout burst into flames.
>
> Engaged another EA, which was turning towards me on the same level. Fired several short bursts at this machine whilst circling. This EA went into a spin, and disappeared from the fight.

with him—just the two of us—and I don't quite know where we got to, but I saw him waggle his wings and dive, and I followed him. Then suddenly he zoomed up and I found a Hun—a two-seater—right in my sights. He'd already given the Hun a burst. He's the most unselfish man I ever met.[65]

Mannock's generosity with younger pilots became legendary. He would first attack and damage the opponent, then veer aside to allow his companion to finish him off and take credit for the kill. Ira Jones wrote, "It is

wonderful how cheered a pilot becomes after he shoots down his first machine; his morale increases by at least a hundred per cent. This is why Mick gives Huns away—to raise the morale of the beginner."[66] Superior officers concluded that Mannock set up at least twenty-five kills for other pilots that he could have taken for himself.

Impressive Character

Mannock could be tough when needed. He demanded strict discipline when flying as a unit and ordered no one to break formation unless they experienced engine trouble. One time a pilot left the group and started maneuvering about the sky, showing off his talents, but quickly scurried back to the pack when Mannock suddenly appeared on his rear and fired a few rounds in his direction.

No one doubted Mannock's courage, for he shot down an impressive number of enemy aircraft while never shying from a battle. Ira Jones recalled that a pilot named Clements owed his life to Mannock's audacity. On May 25, 1918, the pair flew patrol when they spotted a large formation of German aircraft heading their way. Mannock instantly charged toward the group, then noticed that three or four German fighters had surrounded Clements. Mannock broke off his own attack and purposely flew close to the German fighters to draw them away from Clements so his comrade could fly to safety.

"Clements says it was a rotten sight to see one SE [British aircraft] being attacked by such a bunch, and that had it been anyone except Mick, he would have been anxious about his safety," wrote Jones. "We all believe that no Hun will ever shoot down Mick."[67]

Mannock put his craft into such a severe dive that the Germans thought he was about to crash. At four thousand feet Mannock leveled his craft and flew away from the Germans, who had eased off in anticipation of watching their foe smash into the ground.

Four days later Mannock exhibited another display when he charged twelve German fighters over Lille, France, near the Belgian border. Though vastly outnumbered, Mannock knocked down two German planes before retiring to safety.

Mannock's feats stood out in a field where impressive actions occurred on a daily basis. He contended that in a battle the best move for a pilot was to dive at an angle so the opponent's top wing partially blocked his vision. If Mick then missed in that attempt, he preferred to roll under the German's tail and attack from that angle. One British flier, Van Ira, watched Mannock challenge a German fighter in a dogfight that approached a ballet for its beauty and graceful movements.

First, they waltzed around one another like a couple of turkey cocks, Mick being tight on his adversary's tail. The Pfalz [German aircraft] half rolled and fell a few hundred feet beneath him. Mick followed, firing as soon as he got in position.

The Hun then looped—Mick looped too, coming out behind and above his opponent and firing short bursts. The Pfalz then spun—Mick spun also, firing as he spun. The Hun eventually pulled out; Mick was fast on his tail—they were now down to 4,000 feet. The Pfalz now started twisting and turning, which was a sure sign of "wind-up [desperate manuevers to get away]!" After a sharp burst close up, Mick adminis-

To boost morale, Mannock would often setup a kill during combat for his young fliers.

tered the coup de grace [killing], and the poor fellow went down headlong and crashed. A really remarkable exhibition of cruel, cool, calculated Hun-strafing. A marvelous show.[68]

In three months with No. 74 Squadron, Mannock shot down thirty-six enemy aircraft. Each time, he filed a brief combat report that barely mentioned anything except the location and the result. Mannock did not believe in boasting.

"He Needed to Kill"

Normally he kept his feelings bottled up. That is, except when it came to killing Germans. Mannock bore an intense, almost personal hatred for the enemy that extended far beyond that of other Allied pilots. If a member of his squadron were shot down, Man-

It was not enough for Mannock to fight and down planes like this German two-seater "Fokker Wolf"; he possessed an insatiable appetite to kill Germans.

nock immediately jumped into his aircraft and sought revenge, and when he downed a German aircraft he was known to gush, "Sizzle, sizzle—I sent one of the bastards to hell in flames today!"[69]

From wherever the bitterness came—his bleak childhood, his time as a German prisoner in Turkey, possibly—fighting took on a more personal aspect for this British pilot. One of his comrades said, "Fighting wasn't enough for him—he needed to kill."[70]

A pilot named Caldwell watched Mannock finish off a German, and later wrote an account of the stunning episode.

The Hun crashed, but not badly, and most people would have been content with this—but not Mick Mannock. He dived half-a-dozen times at the machine, spraying bullets at the pilot and the observer, who were still showing signs of life. I witnessed this business and flew alongside Mick, yelling at the top of my voice and warning him to stop. On being questioned as to his wild behavior after we had landed, he heatedly replied, "The swines are better dead—no prisoners for me!"[71]

Mannock's bitterness extended even to the valiant Manfred von Richthofen, Germany's Red Baron. When another British pilot once praised Richthofen and raised his glass in a toast, Mannock refused to join in. After learning of Richthofen's death, Mannock stated that he hoped the man had roasted all the way down to earth.

In a macabre ritual followed by many pilots, Mannock retrieved souvenirs from most of his kills and mailed them home. In August 1917 he sent a letter to Jim Eyles, stating,

I sent the parcel off to you yesterday. Pilot's boots which belonged to a dead pilot. Goggles belonging to another. The cigarette holder and case were given to me by the captain observer of a two-seater I brought down. The piece of fabric with a number on it is from another Hun two-seater. The other little brown packet is a field dressing carried by a Hun observer for dressing wounds when in the air.[72]

While Mannock took to his aircraft with hatred and bitterness, he did not look down on any pilot who showed fear. Quite the opposite—he respected anyone who still entered combat even though frightened. The only men who disgusted him were those few who allowed fear to keep them from taking part in combat. One time when that happened to a man in his squadron, Mannock ripped off the pilot's wings in disgust and made him sew a piece of yellow cloth in their place.

He did admit to one overriding concern, which many top aces shared—the fear of death from fire. Before each flight Mannock checked his revolver to make sure it was loaded and working properly, for he swore that "I'll put a bullet through my head if the machine catches fire. They'll never burn me."[73]

Combat Fatigue

Mannock, like most aviators, showed frequent signs of weariness as the number of his encounters rose. In his book *The First Air War, 1914–1918*, historian Lee Kennett describes the unique form of combat fatigue suffered by World War I pilots.

The sheer physical fatigue that came from flying could quickly wear a man down, something not easy to understand for those of us who fly cosseted in the passenger cabin of a jet liner. First of all there was the thunderous, deafening noise of a motor three or four feet away, running at full regime with no trace of a muffler. Then there was the gale-force wind in one's face, laced with engine fumes if the motor were in front, and with a spray of castor oil if it were a rotary; at altitude the stream of air was glacial, and the open, unheated cockpit offered little protection. The aviator's seat was a primitive wicker affair, and it was not adjustable. After two or three hours of such flying, it would sometimes be all a man could do to climb out of the cockpit. Then there was the stress that came from frequent brushes with violent death.

"O! For a Fortnight in the Country!"

Despite displaying incredible bravery, as the war went on Mannock exhibited those same telltale signs of nervous exhaustion that hounded most fighter pilots. The continual grind of daily combat wore down even the hardiest of men, and Mannock proved to be no exception.

He frequently alluded to nerves in his diary. The first mention occurred on April 20, 1917, shortly after he arrived in France, when his engine failed three times in one mission.

Now I can understand what a tremendous strain to the nervous system active service flying is. However cool a man may be there must always be more or less of a tension on the nerves under such trying conditions. When it is considered that seven out of ten forced landings are practically "write-offs" [deaths], and 50 per cent are cases where the pilot is injured, one can understand the strain of the whole business. [74]

The references continued throughout the year and into 1918. On May 6 he recorded that two pilots had left for England because their nerves were shattered, and he wondered who would be next. Twelve days later he wrote that he felt fortunate to still be alive, and on June 14 he added, "Feeling nervy and ill during the last week. Afraid I am breaking up. Captain Keen very decent. Let me off some flying for today. I think I'll take a book and wander into the woods this afternoon. O! for a fortnight [14 days] in the country at home!" [75]

While on a mission in July, he landed after shooting down an aircraft. When he ran up to inspect the German machine, he noticed that he had not only killed the pilot and badly wounded the observer, but had killed a black-and-white terrier dog that was in the plane as a companion. "I felt exactly like a murderer," Mannock confided to his diary. "This sort of thing, together with the strong graveyard stench and the dead and mangled body of the pilot combined to upset me for a few days."[76]

By the summer of 1918 the strain on Mannock was obvious to others. His hatred deepened, and he spent more time alone than usual. He wrote his sister in that month,

Things are getting a bit intense just lately and I don't quite know for how long my nerves will last out. I am rather old now, as airmen go, for fighting. Still, one hopes for the best. These times are so horrible that occasionally I feel life is not worth hanging on to myself. I am supposed to be going home on leave on the nineteenth of this month (if I live long enough) and I shall call at Birmingham to see you all.[77]

In addition to his mental deterioration, Mannock claimed he was having premonitions of his own death. He made even more of a point of checking his revolver before each flight, and he constantly mentioned the large number of men—Allied and German—he had watched plunge to fiery deaths. Mannock even stopped boasting of Germans dying in agony whenever he shot one down. One day after watching a German flutter to the ground and explode, he angrily mentioned to a fellow pilot, "That damn Hun in flames. Why the hell haven't we got parachutes?"[78]

After Mannock shot down his seventy-second airplane, another aviator claimed that England would host an immense pa-

rade for him after the war. Exhausted and worn out, Mannock muttered, "There won't be any 'after the war' for me."[79]

When he visited the Eyles in June, Jim Eyles worried that Mannock was in no condition to return to battle. Mannock cried much of the time and appeared weary every moment. Eyles attempted to talk Mannock into asking for extra leave, but the pilot refused.

His reign with No. 74 Squadron came to an end in July 1918, when Mannock was promoted to major and named commander of No. 85 Squadron. He so loved his time with No. 74 that Mannock, a terror in the skies, cried like a baby on learning the news.

"Shot My Major Down in Flames"

The end came quickly for Mannock. On July 26, 1918, only days after joining No. 85 Squadron, Mannock took off with 2d Lt. D.C. Inglis. As Inglis later explained, Mannock attacked a German airplane, damaged it, then veered away so Inglis could finish the job. Inglis shot down the aircraft, and the two dropped to a lower altitude to check on the destroyed plane. Suddenly, heavy ground fire greeted the pair. Inglis recalled:

I saw Mick start to kick his rudder and realized we were fairly low, then I saw a flame come out of the side of his machine; it grew bigger and bigger. His nose dropped slightly and he went into a slow right-hand turn around about twice, and hit the ground in a burst of flame. I circled at about twenty feet but could not see him, and as things were

Mannock died claiming seventy-three victories in the air.

Like most other aces of the war who eventually succumbed in battle, Mannock's fellow pilots grieved the loss of a gifted aviator. An officer wrote to Mannock's brother,

> Please accept the deepest sympathy from a whole squadron mourning a brave man and the best of comrades. There was no man or officer in the squadron but loved him for his bravery, for his cheerfulness, for his skill, for his patience in teaching others, and for his personality, which made him at once the most efficient and the most popular Commanding Officer in France.[81]

getting hot, made for home. Poor Mick, the bloody bastards had shot my major down in flames.[80]

Mannock's body was never retrieved. Supposedly his airplane had crashed in the midst of terrain that was being heavily shelled by British artillery. The ensuing bombardment obliterated all traces of both Mannock and his airplane.

Mannock died after accumulating seventy-three victories in the air, a total that would have been much higher had he not handed so many others to younger aviators. Despite his unselfishness, Mannock still compiled more victories than any other British ace and set the war's third-highest record, behind the eighty recorded by Germany's Richthofen and the seventy-five of France's Fonck. On July 18, 1919, the British government posthumously awarded the Victoria Cross to Edward Mannock, citing his courage, skill, sense of duty, and self-sacrifice as reasons for bestowing the honor.

Chapter 6

"The Most Redoubtable Adversary of All"

Before France celebrated the daring accomplishments of René Fonck, another flier was garnering headlines in Paris newspapers. Like many other aviators, he felt at home in the skies. Unfortunately, he also shared another trait with fellow pilots—as the brutal air war stretched on, he got the feeling that he would not see the end to the fighting except in his own death.

A Military Heritage

Born in Paris, France, on December 24, 1894, Georges Guynemer personified the typical stereotype of a World War I flying ace—unflinching courage, willingness to take risks from which others shied, and unbridled confidence in his talents. Most of these qualities emerged as a reaction to his childhood, when the sickly Guynemer, probably suffering from tuberculosis, often could not join his schoolmates in sporting activities. His mother and two sisters coddled and overprotected the young Guynemer on ac-

count of his frailty, and as a result the boy struck some friends as spoiled and argumentative.

While the females in the family may have babied Guynemer, his father instilled patriotism and a deep sense of duty in the boy. The family boasted a proud military heritage that reached back to France's days of glory. Ancestors had marched to the Holy Land a thousand years earlier to battle Moslems in the Crusades. Other forebears included one who fought with the legendary Charlemagne, ruler of France from 768 to 814, another bitterly opposed the leaders of the French Revolution in 1789, and a third served in the armies of Napoleon, France's ruler and conqueror of Europe from 1804 to 1815. Guynemer's father continued the tradition by graduating as an officer from the military academy at St. Cyr, the French equivalent of West Point.

Since Guynemer could not participate in many activities in his early years, he focused his energies on schoolwork. He excelled in mathematics and Latin, and pursued an avid fondness for working with engines. The young boy frequently visited engine factories to learn how the pieces were assembled and to absorb every bit of information he could. He spent hours reading about the adventures of France's top aviators and boasted to classmates that he would one day be a pilot and aircraft designer. By the time he graduated from Stanislaus College in Paris, he announced that he wished to enter the field of engineering.

"My God, Have We Only Children Left?"

Guynemer's engineering career came to a sudden halt in August 1914 when his nation declared war on Germany and entered World War I. Not surprisingly, because of his family's military heritage, Guynemer was one of the first to appear at a recruiting center. His childhood ailment still lingered enough that he failed the physical examination. Embarrassed and disappointed, Guynemer tried three more times in a few months, but failed on each attempt.

Guynemer, confident that his tuberculosis was under control and would be no problem, refused to quit. He turned to family friends, especially Captain Bernard-Thierry, an associate of his father's who commanded an aviation school in France. Bernard-Thierry respected Guynemer's determination to serve his nation, and when Guynemer demonstrated his vast knowledge of engines, the officer agreed to accept him as a student mechanic.

The position occupied a low status in the world of aviation—certainly nowhere near that of pilot or observer—but Guynemer was pleased to be able to continue his family's proud tradition of serving the nation in times of crisis. He used the time to study airplanes and engines. He talked with pilots about their tactics and missions, and he read manuals about airplane performance. Maybe he could not yet join the other men

Georges Guynemer was beginning a career in engineering when World War I began. His family's military history prompted him to enlist.

in the air, but he intended to be ready when the time came.

He only had to wait a few months as it turned out. His father contacted old friends in the military—most of them generals by then—and convinced them to add his son's name to those being sent to flight training school. Guynemer started his training on February 1, 1915, and showed such prowess with the airplane that he soloed within five weeks. The other students claimed that Guynemer seemed at home in the cockpit, and he always appeared to know how to fix any mechanical problem.

In June 1915, Guynemer reported to *Escadrille MS3* at Vauciennes in eastern France for his first combat assignment. He initially flew a two-seater Morane Saulnier Parasol aircraft on artillery observation duties, a plane that most pilots considered unreliable and hard to handle. Guynemer shrugged off the plane's reputation and took off without a thought. Not only did the talented pilot experience no difficulties with the plane, but to ensure that his observer brought back the most accurate photographs and information on enemy positions, he dropped to lower altitudes, a move considered risky for any man in any aircraft.

Alarmed superiors warned Guynemer to be more careful. His commanding officer said, "Be a little more cautious. Take a good look round and size up the situation before you make a move, and when you're in the air never, never take unnecessary risks."[82]

The warnings failed to alter Guynemer's daring piloting. On July 19, 1915, he

Top Twelve Aces

Manfred von Richthofen led all pilots with eighty kills, but many other aviators on both sides shot down large numbers of aircraft. The table below lists the top three aces for each of four nations.

GERMANY	
1. Manfred von Richthofen	80
2. Ernst Udet	62
3. E. Loewenhardt	53
GREAT BRITAIN	
1. Edward Mannock	73
2. W. A. "Billy" Bishop (Canadian)	72
3. R. Collishaw (Canadian)	60
FRANCE	
1. René Fonck	75
2. Georges Guynemer	54
3. C. Ningesser	45
UNITED STATES	
1. Edward Rickenbacker	26
2. W. Lambert	22
3. F. Gillette	20

recorded his first kill when he spotted a German airplane heading toward Soissons, France. Although he was on observation duty, Guynemer quickly veered his plane toward the German.

As he later recalled:

We followed him, and as soon as he was inside our lines we dived and placed ourselves about fifty metres [*sic*] under and behind him to the left. At our first salvo the Aviatik [German aircraft] lurched and we saw part of the machine break. He replied with rifle fire, one bullet hitting a wing and

With the assistance of his father's old military friends, Guynemer (left) was sent to flight training school in February 1915.

another grazing Guerder's [the observer's] head and hand. At our next shots the pilot slumped down in the cockpit, the observer raised his arms as if in supplication to the sky, and the Aviatik fell straight down in flames between the trenches.[83]

Ecstatic with his triumph, Guynemer landed near a French artillery unit so his observer could relay vital information. Soldiers who had witnessed the aerial battle congratulated Guynemer, and the artillery commander walked up with a bottle of champagne to offer as a victory salute. He halted a few steps

from Guynemer, stared at the man, and wondered how old he was. When Guynemer replied that he was twenty, the colonel exclaimed, "My God, have we only children left to do the fighting?"[84]

"I Am Now in Absolute Control"

Guynemer added to his totals so that by year's end he had destroyed four German airplanes. By that time, however, he had experienced the hazards of his occupation by being shot down for the first time. In September 1915 a German aviator peppered Guynemer's machine and forced him to crash-land in no-man's-land (the strip of unoccupied territory between the Allied and German trenches). Fortunately, French troops poured out of the trenches to rescue Guynemer—who suffered minor injuries—before their German counterparts could arrive on the scene.

His first encounter with injuries caused Guynemer a great amount of anxiety. He knew that some pilots lost their nerve in the air once they had been wounded, and he was worried that he might experience the same phenomenon. After being treated at the hospital, Guynemer wasted little time in returning to the air to see if he still had the required gumption. As a test, Guynemer purposely allowed a German aircraft to attack him. He returned a happy man.

He wrote to his sister:

As long as you have never been wounded, you think that nothing can ever happen to you. But once you are hit a few times, it is different. The Boche attacked and I merely maneuvered; he emptied at least five hundred shots from his guns and I never answered his fire. That is the way to master one's nerves, little sister. Mine now are entirely mastered. I am now in absolute control.[85]

Guynemer became the first French air hero of the war. Women sought his attention whenever he returned home for a brief vacation, and if he walked about Paris, a large crowd usually followed in his footsteps. Newspapers trumpeted his accomplishments. "The young hero cannot stay still," reported one French paper. "He sits down, he gets up, he walks about, he sits down again, all the time telling about his exploits in pieces and snatches, as if he were talking about a football game or a hunting episode."[86]

Guynemer understood that his newfound fame rested on his ability to kill another human being before being killed. One time in Paris, Guynemer barely avoided hitting a woman as he drove a car about town. When he emerged from the automobile to check on the lady, she shouted out, "Assassin!" Guynemer replied, "Madame, you don't know how right you are!"[87] Possibly for that reason, but also out of modesty, Guynemer never wore his medals when on leave.

"I Flick Bullets Away"

Guynemer, by then flying a single-seater fighter airplane, added to his fame in 1916 by raising his total of destroyed enemy aircraft to twenty-five. He usually started his missions in the same manner. Guynemer carefully inspected the airplane, then talked with the plane's mechanic to see if he had experienced any difficulties preparing the machine. He then hopped into the cockpit, at which time he adopted a look that at first startled his ground crew. One man said, "The look on his face was appalling; the glances were like blows."[88] Guynemer, about to head into mortal conflict, was getting mentally set to face the next few hours.

Death Is a Constant Companion

Mannock and four other fliers profiled in this book failed to survive the war. Even those who outlived combat daily felt death's presence during the war, either by witnessing it in the skies or by feeling the pain of a missing squadron mate. Historian Lee Kennett describes death's overwhelming potency in his book *The First Air War, 1914–1918*.

Death was a frequent visitor to the squadrons, where his passage left its mark. The sudden removal of one man from an intimate group of a dozen was often traumatic for the survivors. Sometimes they knew his fate—someone had seen his fall—but often he just failed to come back, and his comrades waited for a telephone call saying he had been obliged to land elsewhere, then for word from army headquarters that he and his plane had been found—then finally for word from the enemy, who was generally scrupulous about such things. And sometimes they never heard, neither plane nor pilot ever being found. For an appreciable time the missing man's things might be left for his return, and no one would sit in "his" chair. Then one day his replacement would arrive.

Just before taking off he waved to his ground crew, who assumed that it meant the pilot would see them later. As the year unfolded, however, Guynemer also meant it as a good-bye in case he did not return.

He then dashed into the skies in search of foes. When he located one, Guynemer favored the straight-on approach in which he charged directly toward the German. He preferred this method to elaborate maneuverings because it placed him in position to hit what he considered the most vulnerable parts of a German airplane—the propeller, engine, radiator, and pilot.

His methods succeeded beyond expectations, and soon the charred remains of

Guynemer soon enjoyed the fame of being the first French air hero of World War I.

German aircraft littered the countryside below where Guynemer flew. On September 23, 1916, he shot down three enemy aircraft within five minutes. Shortly after claiming his third victim, Guynemer felt his plane rattle and flip upside down from a shell explosion. He went into a dangerous spin and lost four thousand feet before regaining enough control to crash-land the aircraft. The only thing that saved Guynemer from serious injury or death was a special harness he had devised that held him in the plane and prevented him from being tossed out.

French infantry rushed to his aid. Suffering only from bruises and a slashed knee, Guynemer hobbled over to the smoking remains of one of his kills and searched through the wreckage. From one of the bodies he retrieved a photograph of a beautiful girl. When he turned the picture over, he found inscribed on the back, "I wish you all the success in the world in your flying. Love, Gretchen."[89] Rather than bother him, the sentimental words meant little to Guynemer, who figured that it was either the German or he who would die in combat.

The story of how Guynemer shot down three opponents in under five minutes quickly spread throughout the French trenches. Soldiers joked that now French chefs would add a new recipe to their cookbooks called "boiled egg a la Guynemer." According to the recipe, the person should "Take an egg. Put it in boiling water when Guynemer goes into action. Wait until he has shot down three aircraft, then remove and eat."[90]

Guynemer recognized more clearly a brutal fact that the soldiers in the trenches overlooked—each mission he flew might be his last. Soldiers wallowing in the miseries of trench warfare day in and day out only noticed that fliers like Guynemer endured a few harrowing moments of combat, then returned to clean bases. Those frightful moments, however, handed men an exhausting challenge.

On March 13, 1916, Guynemer headed to the Verdun sector in northeastern France, scene of the most horrific battle of the war between French and German forces. There he tangled with three German fighters. Two bullets stung his left arm, and metal slivers slashed his cheeks and left eyelid, producing a torrent of blood down his face. Almost blinded by his own blood, Guynemer evaded his pursuers and landed back at his base.

The injuries kept him out of action for four weeks. In the third week of April, though, an impatient Guynemer checked himself out of the hospital and headed back to his unit. As soon as his commanding officer took a look at Guynemer, who still appeared weak, the officer ordered him back for further treatment.

Guynemer eventually survived eight crashes. To others he lived a charmed life, and even he began thinking that the war would not catch up to him. "People can no longer say that I am a weakling," he told

Guynemer courageously entered and fought every battle as though it were his last.

other pilots. "I flick bullets away from me with my finger tips."[91]

An Act of Chivalry

He could often be gracious in the skies. During a mission in 1916 he encountered one of Germany's top pilots, Ernst Udet, who shot down sixty-two Allied aircraft while surviving the war. One reason he outlived Guynemer and other counterparts was due to the chivalry of the French aviator. Each man immediately realized that he was facing a formidable competitor. The pair circled around each other in an attempt to get behind the other's back and shoot him down, for in a single-seater the machine guns only shot forward, and whoever landed on the other's tail had a tremendous advantage.

Infantrymen below watched in fascination as the aces played out their game of death. Guynemer and Udet sometimes passed so close to each other in their circling and swooping that each man could clearly see the cockpit and helmeted head of his opponent. In one pass Udet identified the painted emblem on Guynemer's plane and realized that he had challenged France's finest. The German employed every tactic he knew to shake Guynemer, but he could not gain an advantage.

For eight minutes the foes traded move with move until Guynemer suddenly looped, flipped over on his back, and flew directly over Udet's head. As the Frenchman passed by, Udet tried to fire, but his gun jammed. Udet attempted to free the stuck bullets by smacking his machine gun with his hands, but nothing worked.

Guynemer alighted on the German's tail and had Udet at his mercy. Instead of shooting down his gallant foe, though, Guynemer waved that he understood Udet's problem and turned away. He could not bring himself to shoot down a helpless pilot, especially one who had put up such a valiant fight.

More accolades came to Guynemer as the war continued. On February 18, 1917, he was promoted to captain, and when in June of that year he recorded his forty-fifth victory, Guynemer received a citation for bravery. The award read:

> One of the elite, a fighter pilot as skillful as he is audacious, he has rendered brilliant service to his country, as much by the number of his victories as by the daily example of his unchanging keenness and evergrowing mastery. Heedless of danger he has become for the enemy, by the sureness of his methods and by the precision of his maneuvers, the most redoubtable adversary of all.[92]

Fatalistic Premonitions

Guynemer loved flying in an aggressive manner, but he knew that he tempted fate by being so reckless. Enemy bullets had already found his airplane on more than a few occasions, he had survived eight crashes, and the odds stated that sooner or later a bullet would inflict fatal damage to him or his machine. Like other pilots, he had a foreboding of things to come. One day he confided to fellow pilot Jean Constantin, "I have got away with it for too long. I have a feeling that one of these days I am not going to come back."[93]

These feelings deepened in the summer of 1917 as he saw other pilots drop to their deaths. He mentioned to many that he thought he would shoot down fifty aircraft, then be killed soon afterward. When he notched his fiftieth victory in August 1917, he told friends in Paris that they would probably not see him again. Close friends noticed a marked deterioration in Guynemer's attitude, and Guynemer disclosed to a Catholic priest that he thought his next mission would be his last.

Guynemer's father worried about his son's depressed mood, apathy, and weariness. He begged Georges to rest more or ask for a transfer to a training division, but his son would not hear of it. His family, after all, had performed its duty to France for one thousand years, and he would not be the one to shirk such a time-honored responsibility.

Few men could bear the burden Guynemer and other pilots assumed. In a two-month span in 1916, for instance, Guynemer engaged in 388 aerial battles, shot down 36 German planes and 3 observation balloons, and forced another 36 damaged German

aircraft to land. The only question remaining was, would shattered nerves, a German bullet, or the end of the war terminate his illustrious career.

Guynemer wagered on the bullet. At a party held in his honor during a visit home, a woman praised the aviator's string of triumphs and asked what honor yet remained for him to win. "The wooden cross,"[94] he replied, referring to the simple marker that would rest above his grave.

Guynemer appeared more nervous than usual as he walked to his airplane on September 11, 1917. He was assigned to fly with

Guynemer in his Nieuport fighter went missing in action on September 11, 1917.

three other men, but when two were detained he and Lieutenant Bozon-Verduraz took off. The pair engaged in a dogfight with a German two-seater, but only Bozon-Verduraz returned. He explained later that they both made a pass and fired thirty rounds at the two-seater, but Bozon-Verduraz had to break off and hasten home when he spotted eight German fighters fast approaching. He never saw Guynemer again. No one knows whether the French pilot failed to see the eight fighters, or whether ground fire or mechanical failure damaged his airplane, but the man was never again seen.

Later that afternoon a French infantry unit relayed a message to Guynemer's airfield informing authorities that they had witnessed a French aircraft plunging into German-held territory. No one could tell if this was Guynemer's plane, so hopes remained high that he was alive. His fellow pilots did not worry too much since Guynemer had a habit of heading out on his own and returning late from missions. One French magazine claimed that he was safely in German hands as a prisoner, while another comforted readers by stating, "Guynemer they say is dead. Guynemer dead! Bah! Those who would believe that don't know him!"[95]

"He Belonged to the Skies"

People crowded French churches to say prayers for the missing hero, and schoolchildren started classes with prayers for his safe return. French president Georges Clemenceau pronounced Guynemer a national hero whose loss would be too hard to bear. If Guynemer were indeed dead, Clemenceau promised swift vengeance.

The French president and the nation received an answer on September 14. A German newspaper announced that a German pilot, Captain Wissemann, had shot down the French ace in combat across the French border near Poelcapelle, Belgium. Details came slowly after that, but within a month the French people learned what had happened to Guynemer. A German doctor and some soldiers located Guynemer's wrecked aircraft, discovered Guynemer with a bullet to the head and his left index finger shot off, but had to depart before retrieving the body due to heavy artillery shelling. The barrage obliterated all traces of Guynemer and his airplane.

Celebrated flier René Fonck carried out Clemenceau's promise of vengeance. Upon hearing the news of Guynemer's death,

The Loss of Guynemer

Georges Guynemer was beloved by both the French nation and his fellow aviators. One who eventually topped his record number of kills, René Fonck, mourned as much as anyone. He records the reaction to Guynemer's death in his memoir, *Ace of Aces*.

In prose and in verse, others have praised his exploits and expressed the grief of the entire country. Parliament voted him the Honors of the Pantheon. But the finest mark of admiration and regret is that which remains forever engraved in the hearts of his comrades-in-arms, each of whom made himself his avenger. Unfortunately, all too many of them fell in this attempt.

At the age of twenty-two, Guynemer died having achieved fifty-three kills and receiving twenty-six citations for bravery.

Fonck jumped into his aircraft, hunted down a German two-seater, and pumped bullets into the fuselage and pilot. As the air-craft flipped over, the observer fell out, and as Fonck later wrote, "He passed only a few meters from my left wing, his arms franti-cally clutching at the emptiness."[96]

French officials engraved Guynemer's name on a plaque and hung it in a Paris crypt reserved for the greats of France. The inscription read, "Fallen on the field of honor on September 11th, 1917—a leg-endary hero, fallen in glory from the sky af-ter three years of fierce struggle."[97]

The twenty-two-year-old Guynemer died after shooting down fifty-three enemy air-planes and amassing twenty-six citations for bravery. Since no one recovered his body, leg-ends abounded that Guynemer actually had not perished but was languishing in a prison camp, or that he would one day suddenly ap-pear as if by magic. Schoolchildren chanted that "He flew so high, on and on in the sky, that he could never come to earth again."[98]

A Catholic cardinal may have said it best. At a packed memorial service for Guynemer, the cardinal stated, "He belonged to the skies and the skies have taken him."[99]

Chapter 7

"Rick Rarely Missed"

The United States did not enter World War I until three years of stalemate in the trenches had passed by, but the nation contributed to ultimate Allied victory with immense land campaigns and a large infusion of air power. One of the men who journeyed across the Atlantic Ocean combined the American infatuation for machines and speed with stirring gallantry and bold leadership. Eddie Rickenbacker, the American "ace of aces," emerged as the United States' most renowned aviator.

Attracted to Speed

Edward Vernon Rickenbacker was born in Columbus, Ohio, on October 8, 1890, to German immigrant parents, William and Elizabeth. The third of eight children, Eddie early displayed a rebellious streak. He smoked cigarettes and headed a gang of youths called the Horsehead Gang, which was really little more than a conglomeration of local boys who pulled pranks. One of those indiscretions almost caused Eddie's death when a large cart flipped over on the boy and cut his leg to the bone. Rickenbacker later claimed that he emerged from his rambunctious childhood as a decent individual because of his father's strict application of family rules. Rickenbacker may have gravitated toward trouble, but he also learned to respect his elders and help out around the house.

He lost his stabilizing influence at age thirteen when his father died in a construction accident. The tragedy forced Rickenbacker to leave school to help support the large family. He worked the night shift at a local glassworks factory for $3.50 per week, and labored in a steel foundry and a shoe factory.

It was his work for a fledgling automobile business that introduced Rickenbacker to cars and speed. In 1906, Lee Frayer, a race car driver and head of an automobile company, hired Rickenbacker as an auto mechanic. The youth proved so adept at fixing engines that Frayer gradually expanded his responsibilities, and before long Rickenbacker started racing cars. Within four years he had won races and gained the label "the Wild Teuton" from newspapers, especially when he established a new land-speed record of 134 miles per hour in 1914. Now associated with stellar automobile concerns like the Peugeot Motor Company of Paris, the Maxwell Motor Company, and the Firestone Tire Company, Rickenbacker earned as much as thirty-five thousand dollars a year racing cars.

In 1916, Rickenbacker visited England on automotive business. While there, Scot-

Edward Vernon Rickenbacker became the most decorated American pilot during World War I.

land Yard agents inspected his luggage and ripped open his clothes searching for secret messages, for they were convinced that Rickenbacker, with German blood in his family, was a spy for Germany. British authorities even detained Rickenbacker for a time, stripped him, and spread lemon juice on his skin to see if any hidden messages had been imprinted on him.

Undeterred, when Rickenbacker returned to the United States he urged the government to organize a squadron of pilots from racing car drivers. He had taken his first ride in an airplane that same year while preparing for an automobile race, and Rickenbacker was convinced that other racers would eagerly join such a unit. The government declined his offer, stating that the nation was not at war and that Rickenbacker, at age twenty-six, was too old.

Off to Europe

Rickenbacker did not have to wait long to join the fighting. After the United States declared war on Germany in April 1917, he enlisted and was assigned as a driver to the staff of Gen. John J. Pershing, the top-ranking American officer in Europe. Rickenbacker came to the attention of one of the earliest advocates of airpower, Col. William "Billy" Mitchell, who believed that the race car driver would have a natural aptitude for flying and whose name might bring in other top quality individuals. Mitchell had Rickenbacker transferred to flight school, where Rickenbacker proved Mitchell's trust by earning his wings in only seventeen days.

In March 1918, Rickenbacker headed to his first assignment, an airfield near Villeneuve southeast of Paris, to fly with the members of the Ninety-Fourth Aero Pursuit Squadron. Although everyone marveled at his expertise with engines—he could diagnose a malfunctioning part in no time simply by listening to the engine sounds—Rickenbacker did not at first fit in with the other fliers, most of whom had graduated from college. An aviator who became one of Rickenbacker's closest friends, Reed Chambers, said, "Rickenbacker was about the most unpopular man alive in those early days. He was big, older, tough as nails. His race track vernacular [language], his profane vocabulary, didn't set right with the cream of American colleges."[100]

Rickenbacker shrugged off these initial reactions and focused on preparing for combat. He was disappointed in that area as well, for the United States had yet to adequately arm its air squadrons. Old planes and a lack of spare parts hampered their training, but the men made the best of a poor situation.

At first, Rickenbacker (center) did not fit in with other members of the Ninety-Fourth Pursuit Squadron.

"We were one disappointed group of fighter pilots," Rickenbacker wrote after the war. "The planes we found waiting for us were old Nieuports cast off by the French. Even that was not the worst of it. The planes had no guns. And the pilots of the 95th Squadron had never been through gunnery training."[101]

"I Had Passed My First Test"

Rickenbacker's first mission proved to be a true learning experience. His squadron leader, noted American ace Raoul Lufbery, announced that he intended to take two men along on a mission over German lines. The pilots, eager to head into battle, lined up to hear who the fortunate two would be. Lufbery selected Rickenbacker and Douglas Campbell.

To the envy of the remaining squadron members, on March 6, 1918, Rickenbacker and Campbell followed Lufbery into the skies. Rickenbacker thought of a war poster he had seen in the United States picturing a pretty girl standing near huge letters urging citizens to either fight or support the war effort through purchasing bonds. With the enemy only miles away, Rickenbacker smiled and figured he had no choice now.

German fighters were not Rickenbacker's first problem. Air currents so heavily buffeted his aircraft that Rickenbacker feared he would become airsick. The rookie aviator clenched his teeth and prayed that he not throw up all over his cockpit, but German antiaircraft fire shook him out of his potential ailments. The specter of death dwarfed the possibility of becoming airsick, and Rickenbacker flew the rest of the mission without thinking about the malady. "A feeling of elation surged through me," recalled Rickenbacker. "I had been fired at, and I had kept my wits about me. The flight home was one of my most exquisite flying experiences. I had passed my first test."[102]

When the trio landed, Lufbery let his excited rookie pilots boast to their comrades about the mission. They discussed every detail, laying heavier emphasis on the exploding shells. When their squadron mates asked if they had seen any German aircraft, both Rickenbacker and Campbell claimed to have spotted none.

With a wry smile and knowing look, Lufbery stepped in to explain that they had not only not seen one German plane, but had passed a total of fifteen different aircraft, none of which either inexperienced aviator had seen. Rickenbacker realized that he had much to learn about this new style of warfare before he could even approximate the talent of men like Lufbery.

Battling Airsickness

Rickenbacker made a point of learning something from each of his flights, whether it had to do with speed, angle of approach, or how to handle wind currents. He realized that many pilots did not live long enough to gain the knowledge of a man like Lufbery, but he was determined to absorb whatever he could each time he took off.

He almost joined the lengthy list of aviators who died before they had an opportunity to make a name for themselves. Twice during that first month he barely escaped being shot down. The first time a French pilot, erroneously thinking Rickenbacker's craft was German, attacked. Rickenbacker had to utilize every bit of skill to turn his airplane on its side so the French airman would see the U.S. insignia. On the second occasion Rickenbacker attacked a solitary German fighter, but wondered why the opponent did not seem too concerned about the American's approach. Suddenly recalling Lufbery's advice to watch out for traps, Rickenbacker turned back to see three German fighters bearing down on his tail. Few pilots escaped death in such situations, but Rickenbacker flew into a large cloud bank and evaded the pursuers.

Rickenbacker pushed himself in ways that other pilots avoided. To eliminate the problem with airsickness he had experienced on his first flight, Rickenbacker purposely ate food, then immediately went into the air and put his airplane into hard twists and turns. He would throw up, land, eat more food while his crew cleaned the aircraft, then head once more into the sky. He repeated this procedure day after day until he finally could take off and fly without getting sick.

"I Was an Automaton Behind the Gun Barrels"

After a while the men of the Ninety-Fourth Aero Pursuit Squadron forged tight bonds. As a symbol of their unit pride, the men discussed various possibilities for insignias to be painted on the sides of their aircraft. They considered different suggestions until the flight surgeon mentioned the American custom of accepting a challenge by throwing a hat into the ring. The men agreed to have such an emblem adopted, and from then on the unit was known as the Hat-in-the-Ring Squadron.

Rickenbacker recorded his first kill on April 29, 1918. He and James Norman Hall were patrolling over German lines when they spotted an enemy aircraft. Hall pounced on the German while Rickenbacker remained at a higher altitude to cut off whatever escape route the foe adopted. When the German tried to elude Hall, Rickenbacker shot him down.

The death did not bother Rickenbacker. He wrote in his autobiography, "I had no regrets over killing a fellow human being. I do not believe that at that moment I even considered the matter. Like nearly all air fighters, I was an automaton behind the gun barrels of my plane. I never thought of killing an individual but of shooting down an enemy plane."[103]

The Thrill of the Chase

Rickenbacker had an edge in combat that his fellow pilots and foes lacked. His extensive racing experience in automobiles had accustomed him to living with danger, to pushing man and machine to the limits, to knowing when to ask for that extra ounce of performance. At the right moment—usually much closer to the enemy than most pilots allowed—Rickenbacker unleashed an accurate salvo of bullets into the target that eliminated it from the battle.

Reed Chambers claimed that Rickenbacker changed when he headed into action. Rickenbacker, he wrote,

> couldn't put as many holes in a [practice] target that was being towed [across the sky] as I could, but he could put more holes in a target that was shooting at him than I could. Rickenbacker's greatest asset was his judgment of distance. He could move right in on them, and he wouldn't shoot until he could see the whites of their eyes. I and many others, we'd start shooting too far away, and our guns would jam or they'd splatter so wide that we didn't get them. But Rick rarely missed. [104]

Rickenbacker thrilled at the prospect of encountering a talented German and going one-on-one with a qualified foe. He told family members that after seeing each other, fliers often maneuvered about like dancers in the sky to determine the skill level of their opponent and to gain an advantageous position from which to attack. If neither could gain the upper hand, they frequently waved to one another, broke off the engagement, and flew away.

In the early days of fighting, each mission offered excitement and adventure—until a man lost a close friend. That

Rickenbacker, pictured here with his plane.

occurrence shoved death front and center and made each man realize that any day could be his last. Rickenbacker and Chambers still lusted for combat, but they added a routine after some of their war buddies had been killed—before each mission they shook hands as if they were never going to see one another again.

89

In September 1918, Rickenbacker became commander of the Ninety-Fourth Aero Pursuit Squadron.

A Close Call

Like anyone else, Rickenbacker had his share of close calls. One time as he neared a German airfield, Rickenbacker cut back on the engine so his airplane would silently glide toward the enemy without alerting them. For a few moments he stalked the airfield, then watched three German aircraft take off, blissfully unaware that Rickenbacker was waiting for them. He maneuvered into position behind the last of the three and from fifty yards peppered the German aircraft with accurate fire.

Just then he heard bullets tear into his plane and saw that his top right wing had suddenly collapsed. As the fabric ripped away, the plane flipped over on its right side and the tail swung up, sending Rickenbacker into what appeared to be an uncontrollable spin. "With the nose down, the tail began revolving to the right, faster and faster," he later wrote. "It was death. I had not lost my willingness to fight to live, but in that situation there was not much that I could do. Even birds need two wings to fly."[105]

The two German aircraft continued firing bullets toward Rickenbacker as the American spun madly toward the ground. Rickenbacker recalled the good times he had enjoyed in his life, said a quick prayer, then reached down to open the throttle in a last ditch attempt to right the craft. The move added power to the airplane, lifted the nose, and gave Rickenbacker enough control that he could nurse the plane back toward friendly territory. Rickenbacker miraculously survived heavy German antiaircraft fire at only two thousand feet, then approached his airfield barely above treetop level because of the weakened state of the aircraft. To avoid losing power and crashing, Rickenbacker brought his plane in at top speed and trusted he would not run out of room before the plane stopped. At the end of the hectic ride, Rickenbacker stepped out of the plane, wobbled over to his crew, then collapsed.

He endured that incident, but most of his cohorts did not return. So many pilots from the Ninety-Fourth died in May and June 1918 that only Rickenbacker, Chambers, and one other flier remained from the unit that had formed only a few months earlier. Most had perished when flames engulfed their aircraft.

Battling the Balloons

Rickenbacker attributed that dismal period in part to attacks against German observation balloons. He claimed that they proved more dangerous than enemy fighters because, to successfully approach a balloon, a pilot had to maintain course at the same altitude as the balloons. Since the Germans already knew the balloon's altitude, they could set their antiaircraft shells to explode at that exact level. Antiaircraft guns ringed each balloon as well, meaning an American flier had to attack through one ring, get at the balloon, then exit a second ring on the other side. If a pilot survived the attack, he then had to fend off the inevitable group of German fighters that invariably protected balloons.

"Death by burning was the death we dreaded more than any other," claimed Rickenbacker, echoing the sentiments of most World War I aviators. "Our planes were constructed of wooden frameworks covered with fabric. The fabric was treated with 'dope,' a highly combustible fluid that drew up the cloth and stretched it tight."[106]

Reflections from a Hospital Bed

Rickenbacker was confined to a hospital in June not because of a battle wound but due to a severe ear infection. While there he reflected on his previous experiences and decided that he had made too many mistakes in judgment. He concluded that if he were to survive, he had to eliminate

"The Heaviest Burden"

Eddie Rickenbacker bore numerous burdens during the war, but possibly none had the enormous impact of his being named American "ace of aces" after his seventh victory. Normally a person is thrilled at the prospect of being number one, but as Rickenbacker explains in his memoir of the war, *Fighting the Flying Circus*, it was a mixed blessing.

Mingled with this natural desire to become the leading fighting Ace of America was a haunting superstition that did not leave my mind until the very end of the war. It was that the very possession of the title—Ace of Aces—brought with it the unavoidable doom that had overtaken all its previous holders. I wanted it and yet I feared to learn that it was mine! In later days I began to feel that this superstition was almost the heaviest burden that I carried with me into the air. Perhaps it served to redouble my caution and sharpened my fighting senses. But never was I able to forget that the life of a title-holder is short.

the errors, which included taking unnecessary risks.

That included checking his ammunition. During one flight Rickenbacker failed to destroy the target when his guns jammed at close range. When he returned to base he and his mechanic discussed the matter and concluded that an oversized shell had caused the malfunction. They agreed to inspect every round before each mission to prevent a repeat.

While in the hospital he dreamed that two of the newer pilots, Walter Smyth and Alexander Bruce, collided in the air. Their wings touched, fell off, and both men plunged to their deaths. When Rickenbacker awoke, another man from his unit was standing near his bed, waiting to hand him the sad news that Smyth and Bruce had died—exactly as Rickenbacker had dreamed.

The deaths infuriated Rickenbacker, for he believed that parachutes could have saved both men, but superiors argued that parachutes would only encourage pilots to jump out of the aircraft too soon. "It was absolutely criminal for our higher command to withhold parachutes from us. Men who could have lived on to serve America both in war and in peace perished in agony because of a lack of a parachute."[107]

In September, Rickenbacker shot down his seventh aircraft to take the lead among active American fliers. He enjoyed the honor as American "ace of aces," but he also realized that four other men had held the title before him. Each man was now dead.

Commander of the Ninety-Fourth

On September 24, Rickenbacker became commander of the Hat-in-the-Ring Squadron after the unit's previous commanding officer had been killed. The first move he made was to gather his pilots and instruct them on how he intended to run the unit. Rickenbacker banned all saluting because he wanted every man—from the commanding officer to the freshest mechanic—to feel like an equal part of the team. He ordered them to check each bullet to avoid guns jamming, and he taught them how to gain extra power from their engines by not using the engine at full power until the precise moment it was needed. He ended by stating that he would lead all missions, and that he would not ask any man to volunteer for a hazardous mission until he had volunteered.

To prove that he intended to back up his words, Rickenbacker headed out alone the very next day, attacked seven German planes, and shot down two. He not only impressed his unit, but received the Congressional Medal of Honor for his exploits. Day after day he led his unit into battle, determined that the Ninety-Fourth gain recognition as America's top squadron.

Reed Chambers recalled that Rickenbacker

always patrolled at just enough rpm's [engine revolutions per minute] to prevent stalling. He saved the ship for the moment he needed it. When he fought, however, he called for maximum power and drove the plane until it nearly fell apart. Most of the pilots he killed never knew what hit them. Out of the sun, a quick burst and gone. That was Rickenbacker.[108]

Working Overtime

According to Chambers, Rickenbacker drove "himself to exhaustion. He'd fly the required patrol. Then he and I would come back to the field, have a cup of coffee, get into our second ships and go hunting by ourselves."[109]

In a September 26, 1918, encounter, Rickenbacker and a daring German charged straight at one another in a deadly game of chicken. As they were about to collide, the German veered off and Rickenbacker flipped over into a loop and rolled the plane so he was on the German's tail. A brief round of firing produced smoke and flames in the enemy aircraft and sent it spiraling to the ground. When Rickenbacker stepped out of his aircraft at the airfield he found bullet holes in his machine, and a bullet had burned a path in the side of his helmet.

Within six weeks the war was over. When news came in on November 11 that the fighting had stopped, members of Rickenbacker's unit overturned tables, shot pistols into the air, and danced in celebration. One pilot kept repeating, "I've lived through the war, I've lived through the war!"[110] Rickenbacker, who finished with twenty-two downed aircraft and four balloons destroyed, wrestled his mechanic to the ground in joy.

"The War Was Over"

The end of the war caused jubilation among pilots of all nations. As the time drew close to the actual end to the fighting, Rickenbacker jumped into a plane and flew over the front lines to view the spectacle. In his autobiography *Rickenbacker*, he recorded the unforgettable sights as he watched weary soldiers emerge from opposing lines.

> From my observer's seat overhead, I watched them throw their helmets in the air, discard their guns, wave their hands. Then all up and down the front, the two groups of men began edging toward each other across no-man's-land. Seconds before they had been willing to shoot each other; now they came forward. Hesitantly at first, then more quickly, each group approached the other. I could see them hugging each other, dancing, jumping. Americans were passing out cigarettes and chocolate. The war was over.

Postwar Enterprises

Rickenbacker returned to the United States a national hero. Offers from car companies poured in, but he declined every opportunity so he could go into an aerial mapping business with Reed Chambers.

He left that in 1921 to organize the Rickenbacker Motor Company, a firm that produced passenger cars. Rickenbacker knew the ins and outs of engines and machines, but his unfamiliarity with financing and organizing a nationwide concern caused severe problems. Within five years the company folded, leaving Rickenbacker saddled with a debt of $250,000. He vowed to pay off every penny rather than take what he saw as the easy, but immoral, way out by declaring bankruptcy. True to his word, Rickenbacker eventually repaid every creditor.

Auto racing reentered his life in 1927 when Rickenbacker obtained partial control of the famed Indianapolis Motor Speedway in Indiana. Although he combined this work with other ventures, such as joining the Cadillac Motor Car Company in 1928, Rickenbacker remained the speedway's president until 1945.

Rickenbacker never forgot his other passion—aviation. In 1935, now married to Adelaide Durant and the father of two sons, Rickenbacker joined Eastern Airlines. He gradually worked his way up through the ranks until he served as its president, where his wise business moves placed Eastern on sound financial footing. In 1953, Rickenbacker became the company's chairman of the board.

Airman Forever

The World War I aviator used his wartime status to promote aviation throughout the country. He flew to most major cities to convince local officials of the need for airports, and influenced twenty-five to develop such establishments.

During World War II (1941–45), Rickenbacker served the nation in various capacities. He traveled to England, North Africa, Iran, China, and other locations as a special envoy for the president to inspect aviation fa-

After the war, Rickenbacker pursued various occupations, eventually becoming chairman of the board for Eastern Airlines.

cilities. In October 1942, during one such visit to the South Pacific, Rickenbacker and seven other men spent three weeks floating in rafts after their aircraft crashed into the Pacific Ocean. Rickenbacker took command of the group and maintained order until their rescue on November 13, 1942, off the Ellice Islands, five hundred miles from their intended destination. Rickenbacker lost more than sixty pounds from the ordeal, but he emerged as an even greater hero to his countrymen.

The famed race car driver and aviator continued working until October 1972, when he suffered a stroke. He recovered sufficiently to travel, but while visiting friends in Switzerland, he died on July 23, 1973.

✵ Notes ✵

Introduction: "It Was Like a Sport"

1. Quoted in Lee Kennett, *The First Air War, 1914–1918*. New York: Free Press, 1991, p. 168.
2. Quoted in Kennett, *The First Air War,* p. 156.
3. Quoted in Arthur Gordon, *The American Heritage History of Flight*. New York: American Heritage, 1962, p. 91.
4. Quoted in Kennett, *The First Air War,* p. 148.
5. Quoted in Gordon, *The American Heritage History of Flight,* p. 191.

Chapter 1: The Red Baron

6. Manfred von Richthofen, *The Red Air Fighter*. London: Greenhill Books, 1999, p. 41.
7. Von Richthofen, *The Red Air Fighter,* p. 41.
8. Quoted in Ezra Bowen, *Knights of the Air*. Alexandria, VA: Time-Life Books, 1980, p. 119.
9. Von Richthofen, *The Red Air Fighter,* p. 54.
10. Quoted in Bowen, *Knights of the Air,* p. 119.
11. Quoted in Stephen Longstreet, *The Canvas Falcons: The Men and Planes of World War I*. London: Leo Cooper, 1995, p. 94.
12. Von Richthofen, *The Red Air Fighter,* p. 62.
13. Von Richthofen, *The Red Air Fighter,* p. 76.
14. Quoted in Longstreet, *The Canvas Falcons,* p. 95.
15. Quoted in Longstreet, *The Canvas Falcons,* p. 98.
16. Quoted in Bowen, *Knights of the Air,* p. 118.
17. Von Richthofen, *The Red Air Fighter,* p. 95.
18. Quoted in Longstreet, *The Canvas Falcons,* p. 98.
19. Quoted in Robert Jackson, *Fighter Pilots of World War I*. New York: St. Martin's Press, 1977, p. 44.
20. Quoted in Jackson, *Fighter Pilots of World War I,* p. 47.
21. Quoted in Bowen, *Knights of the Air,* p. 137.
22. Quoted in Bowen, *Knights of the Air,* p. 138.
23. Quoted in Jackson, *Fighter Pilots of World War I,* p. 40.
24. Quoted in Bowen, *Knights of the Air,* p. 139.

Chapter 2: The Child as Killer

25. Quoted in www.times1190.freeserve.co.uk/albert.htm., p. 4.

26. Quoted in www.times1190.freeserve.co.uk/albert.htm., p. 5.

27. Quoted in www.times1190.freeserve.co.uk/albert.htm., p. 1.

28. Quoted in Longstreet, *The Canvas Falcons*, p. 195.

29. Quoted in Bowen, *Knights of the Air*, pp. 96, 98.

30. Quoted in Jackson, *Fighter Pilots of World War I*, p. 66.

31. Quoted in Jackson, *Fighter Pilots of World War I*, p. 66.

32. Quoted in Longstreet, *The Canvas Falcons*, p. 194.

33. Quoted in Kennett, *The First Air War*, p. 170.

34. Quoted in Longstreet, *The Canvas Falcons*, p. 198.

35. Quoted in www.times1190.freeserve.co.uk/albert.htm., p. 19.

Chapter 3: "Ace of Aces"

36. René Fonck, *Ace of Aces*. Garden City, NY: Doubleday, 1967, p. 2.

37. Quoted in Jackson, *Fighter Pilots of World War I*, p. 144.

38. Quoted in Jackson, *Fighter Pilots of World War I*, p. 145.

39. Quoted in Jackson, *Fighter Pilots of World War I*, p. 145.

40. Fonck, *Ace of Aces*, p. 124.

41. Quoted in Bruce Robertson, ed., *Air Aces of the 1914–1918 War*. Los Angeles: Aero Publishers, 1964, p. 61.

42. Quoted in Jackson, *Fighter Pilots of World War I*, p. 143.

43. Quoted in Jackson, *Fighter Pilots of World War I*, p. 149.

44. Quoted in Longstreet, *The Canvas Falcons*, p. 156.

45. Fonck, *Ace of Aces*, p. 87.

46. Quoted in Jackson, *Fighter Pilots of World War I*, p. 152.

Chapter 4: Death on a Picket Fence

47. Quoted in Bowen, *Knights of the Air*, p. 100.

48. Quoted in Thomas R. Funderburk, *The Fighters: The Men and Machines of the First Air War*. New York: Grosset & Dunlap, 1965, p. 166.

49. Quoted in Longstreet, *The Canvas Falcons*, p. 260.

50. Quoted in Longstreet, *The Canvas Falcons*, p. 260.

51. Quoted in Quentin Reynolds, *They Fought for the Sky*. New York: Rinehart 1957, p. 255.

52. Edward V. Rickenbacker, *Rickenbacker*. Englewood Cliffs, NJ: Prentice-Hall, 1967, p. 119.

53. Rickenbacker, *Rickenbacker*, p. 117.

54. Quoted in Funderburk, *The Fighters*, p. 167.

55. Quoted in Rickenbacker, *Rickenbacker*, p. 120.

56. Quoted in Rickenbacker, *Rickenbacker*, p. 117.

57. Quoted in Longstreet, *The Canvas Falcons*, p. 263.

58. Quoted in Rickenbacker, *Rickenbacker*, pp. 127–28.

59. Rickenbacker, *Rickenbacker*, p. 129.

Chapter 5: "No Hun Will Ever Shoot Down Mick"

60. Edward Mannock, *The Personal Diary of Major Edward "Mick" Mannock*, introduced and annotated by Frederick Oughton. London: Neville Spearman, 1966, p. 17.
61. Mannock, *Personal Diary*, p. 147.
62. Mannock, *Personal Diary*, pp. 73, 75.
63. Quoted in Jackson, *Fighter Pilots of World War I*, p. 55.
64. Quoted in Jackson, *Fighter Pilots of World War I*, p. 57.
65. Quoted in Mannock, *Personal Diary*, pp. 190–91.
66. Quoted in Jackson, *Fighter Pilots of World War I*, p. 59.
67. Quoted in Jackson, *Fighter Pilots of World War I*, p. 58.
68. Quoted in Longstreet, *The Canvas Falcons*, pp. 187–88.
69. Quoted in Jackson, *Fighter Pilots of World War I*, p. 56.
70. Quoted in Kennett, *The First Air War*, p. 168.
71. Quoted in Mannock, *Personal Diary*, p. 187.
72. Quoted in Jackson, *Fighter Pilots of World War I*, p. 56.
73. Quoted in Longstreet, *The Canvas Falcons*, p. 186.
74. Mannock, *Personal Diary*, p. 49.
75. Mannock, *Personal Diary*, p. 111.
76. Mannock, *Personal Diary*, p. 119.
77. Quoted in Jackson, *Fighter Pilots of World War I*, p. 60.
78. Mannock, *Personal Diary*, p. 191.
79. Mannock, *Personal Diary*, p. 197.
80. Quoted in Longstreet, *The Canvas Falcons*, p. 190.
81. Quoted in Mannock, *Personal Diary*, p. 203.

Chapter 6: "The Most Redoubtable Adversary of All"

82. Quoted in Jackson, *Fighter Pilots of World War I*, p. 136.
83. Quoted in Jackson, *Fighter Pilots of World War I*, p. 134.
84. Quoted in Reynolds, *They Fought for the Sky*, p. 80.
85. Quoted in Reynolds, *They Fought for the Sky*, p. 201.
86. Quoted in Kennett, *The First Air War*, pp. 155–56.
87. Quoted in Kennett, *The First Air War*, p. 173.
88. Quoted in Reynolds, *They Fought for the Sky*, p. 200.
89. Quoted in Jackson, *Fighter Pilots of World War I*, p. 138.
90. Quoted in Jackson, *Fighter Pilots of World War I*, p. 138.
91. Quoted in Jackson, *Fighter Pilots of World War I*, p. 139.
92. Quoted in Robertson, *Air Aces of the 1914–1918 War*, p. 56.
93. Quoted in Jackson, *Fighter Pilots of World War I*, p. 139.
94. Quoted in Reynolds, *They Fought for the Sky*, p. 202.
95. Quoted in Longstreet, *The Canvas Falcons*, p. 166.

96. Fonck, *Ace of Aces*, p. 70.

97. Quoted in Robertson, *Air Aces of the 1914–1918 War*, p. 55.

98. Quoted in Jackson, *Fighter Pilots of World War I*, p. 142.

99. Quoted in Reynolds, *They Fought for the Sky*, p. ix.

Chapter 7: "Rick Rarely Missed"

100. Quoted in Bowen, *Knights of the Air*, p. 153.

101. Rickenbacker, *Rickenbacker*, p. 117.

102. Rickenbacker, *Rickenbacker*, p. 120.

103. Rickenbacker, *Rickenbacker*, p. 126.

104. Quoted in Gordon, *The American Heritage History of Flight*, p. 194.

105. Rickenbacker, *Rickenbacker*, p. 132.

106. Rickenbacker, *Rickenbacker*, p. 127.

107. Rickenbacker, *Rickenbacker*, p. 142.

108. Quoted in Bowen, *Knights of the Air*, p. 174.

109. Quoted in Bowen, *Knights of the Air*, p. 174.

110. Quoted in Rickenbacker, *Rickenbacker*, p. 158.

☆ Chronology of Events ☆

1885

March 14: Raoul Lufbery is born in France.

1887

May 24: Edward Mannock is born in Aldershot, England.

1890

October 8: Edward "Eddie" Rickenbacker is born in Columbus, Ohio.

1892

May 2: Manfred von Richthofen is born in Breslau, Prussia.

1894

March 27: René Fonck is born in Saulcy-sur-Meurthe, France.

December 24: Georges Guynemer is born in Paris, France.

1896

August 14: Albert Ball is born in Nottingham, England.

1914

June 28: Austrian archduke Franz Ferdinand and his wife are assassinated in Sarajevo, leading most major nations of Europe to declare war.

August 4: Germany invades Belgium, France invades Germany.

August 12: 120,000 British soldiers arrive in France.

1915

February: French pilot Roland Garros mounts a machine gun that fires through the aircraft's propellers.

April: Edward Mannock is returned to England from a detention camp in Turkey.

June: Georges Guynemer reports to *Escadrille MS3* in France.

July: British pilot Lanoe Hawker mounts a rifle on the right side of his aircraft to enable him to fly and shoot at the same time.

July: Raoul Lufbery receives his wings as a member of the French Air Arm.

July 19: Georges Guynemer records his first kill.

1916

February: Albert Ball joins a British squadron in France.

February 21: Battle of Verdun begins.

May 24: Raoul Lufbery joins the *Escadrille Americaine.*

Summer: Great air battles are fought to control the skies over the Verdun and Somme River battlefields.

June 25: Albert Ball records his first kill.

July 1: Battle of the Somme begins.

July 30: Raoul Lufbery records his first kill.

August: Richthofen joins a special air squadron formed by Oswald Boelcke.

September 17: Richthofen records his first kill.

November 18: Battle of the Somme ends.

December 18: Battle of Verdun ends.

1917

January: Richthofen is given command of *Jagdstaffel 11*, the unit that would become the famed Flying Circus.

April: Edward Mannock reports to No. 40 Squadron in France.

April 6: United States declares war on Germany.

April 25: René Fonck joins a fighter squadron.

May 6: Albert Ball records his forty-fourth, and final victory.

May 7: Albert Ball is shot down and killed in battle, Edward Mannock records his first kill.

September 11: Georges Guynemer is killed in battle.

1918

February: Raoul Lufbery joins the American Ninety-Fifth Aero Squadron.

March: Eddie Rickenbacker joins the Ninety-Fourth Aero Pursuit Squadron in France.

April: Raoul Lufbery becomes commander of the Ninety-Fourth Aero Pursuit Squadron.

April 20: Richthofen records his eightieth and final kill.

April 21: Richthofen is killed in combat.

April 29: Eddie Rickenbacker records his first kill.

May 9: René Fonck shoots down six German aircraft in seven minutes.

May 19: Raoul Lufbery is killed in combat.

July 26: Edward Mannock is killed in combat.

September 24: Eddie Rickenbacker is named commander of the Ninety-Fourth Aero Pursuit Squadron.

November 1: René Fonck records his seventy-fifth, and final victory.

November 11: War ends.

1942

November 13: Eddie Rickenbacker is rescued after spending three weeks floating on a raft in the Pacific Ocean.

1953

June 18: René Fonck dies in Paris at the age of fifty-nine.

1973

July 23: Eddie Rickenbacker dies in Switzerland.

⋆ For Further Reading ⋆

Editors of Time-Life Books, *This Fabulous Century: Volume 2, 1910–1920*. New York: Time-Life Books, 1969. This popular history contains an excellent section on World War I, complete with numerous photographs.

Martin Gilbert, *The First World War: A Complete History*. New York: Henry Holt, 1994. Gilbert, author of numerous books on war and European history, has written a serious account of the war. He peppers his valuable work with numerous quotes and poems pertaining to the fighting. Though difficult for early teenagers, the book is a wealth of information for the interested reader.

Richard Goldstein, *Mine Eyes Have Seen*. New York: Simon & Schuster, 1997. Goldstein gathers first-person accounts of major events in American history. His selections for World War I include Alvin York, Harry S. Truman, the war in the skies, and President Woodrow Wilson.

Gene Gurney, *Flying Aces of World War I*. New York: Random House, 1965. Gurney produced a very fine book for students in grades five to eight. In addition to chapters covering the lives of eight top pilots, he includes helpful background on the air war.

Joy Hakim, *An Age of Extremes*. New York: Oxford University Press, 1994. Hakim's ac-

claimed series includes this volume, which depicts the American entry and involvement in World War I.

James Norman Hall, *The Lafayette Flying Corps, Vols. I and II*. Boston: Houghton Mifflin, 1920. Hall, who later gained fame as co-author of the *Bounty* trilogy, has left a fine account of American aviators in the war.

Cecil Lewis, *Sagittarius Rising*. New York: Collier Books, 1936. Lewis has given us one of the war's most memorable memoirs with this book. He provides vivid detail of fighting operations.

S. L. A. Marshall, *The American Heritage History of World War I*. New York: American Heritage, 1964. A distinguished military historian, Marshall has written a complete if not lively account of the war. What sets this book apart from others are the numerous photographs and the unique maps.

Linda R. Monk, ed., *Ordinary Americans: U. S. History Through the Eyes of Everyday People*. New York: Close Up, 1994. Monk's book, similar to Goldstein's, presents seven accounts of Americans who were involved in the war. The book breathes life into the story by relying on first-person accounts.

Robin Prior and Trevor Wilson, *The First World War*. London: Cassell, 1999. Part of a distinguished series of war histories, this book offers a decent summary of the major battles, including material on the air war. Its colorful maps are extremely helpful.

Red Reeder, *The Story of the First World War*. New York: Duell, Sloan and Pearce, 1962. Written by a prolific military historian who specialized in books for the younger market, this volume contains excellent accounts of all aspects of the war.

Edward V. Rickenbacker, *Fighting the Flying Circus*. New York: Frederick A. Stoles, 1919. While Rickenbacker's later autobiography includes a more comprehensive look at the American ace, this book gives a useful glimpse into his war years.

R. R. Sellman, *The First World War*. New York: Criterion Books, 1962. Written for the junior high school market, this easy-to-read book delivers an examination of the war that might be a good place for the uninitiated in World War I to start.

Gail B. Stewart, *World War I*. San Diego: Lu- cent Books, 1991. Numerous photos and sidebars supplement a good basic account of the war. The author has written numerous books for the teenage market, and her expertise shows through.

James L. Stokesbury, *A Short History of World War I*. New York: William Morrow, 1981. Stokesbury, a prolific military historian, delivers a readable, sound account of World War I. Though comparatively brief, the book contains gripping chapters that cover all aspects of the war, both political and military. This book would be an excellent place to start for anyone wanting to learn about the conflict.

Mark Sullivan, *Our Times, The United States, 1900–1925: Volume 5, Over Here 1914–1918*. New York: Charles Scribner's Sons, 1933. Mark Sullivan's multivolume history of the United States has long been a favorite with readers. His lively writing augments the numerous photographs and poems.

☆ Works Consulted ☆

Books

Ezra Bowen, *Knights of the Air.* Alexandria, VA: Time-Life Books, 1980. Bowen has written one of the best accounts of the many fine volumes in Time-Life's series, *The Epic of Flight.* A person of any age would enjoy the beautifully written volume, which is liberally supplemented with photographs and charts.

René Fonck, *Ace of Aces.* Garden City, NY: Doubleday, 1967. The leading Allied aviator of World War I presents his version of the fighting in this classic memoir. Never at a loss for words, Fonck's statements and conclusions delight and entertain the reader.

Thomas R. Funderburk, *The Fighters: The Men and Machines of the First Air War.* New York: Grosset & Dunlap, 1965. Funderburk combines decent sketches of the pilots with good descriptions of the aircraft they flew in this helpful volume.

Arthur Gordon, *The American Heritage History of Flight.* New York: American Heritage, 1962. Gordon's superb chapter on the air war during World War I forms only one portion of an exciting book. Anyone with an interest in aviation would love this volume.

Robert Jackson, *Fighter Pilots of World War I.* New York: St. Martin's Press, 1977. Jackson includes biographies of fifteen top aviators from the war, including von Richthofen, Rickenbacker, and the other five men profiled in this book.

Lee Kennett, *The First Air War, 1914–1918.* New York: Free Press, 1991. Kennett's book is an excellent place to start researching World War I aviators. Rather than delivering a compilation of biographies, he portrays the everyday lives of pilots and presents what combat was like for the men. Kennett, an established historian, smoothly incorporates quotations into the text.

Stephen Longstreet, *The Canvas Falcons: The Men and Planes of World War I.* London: Leo Cooper, 1995. While Longstreet offers information on different aviators, the poor writing style and lack of organization make this book difficult to use.

Edward Mannock, *The Personal Diary of Major Edward "Mick" Mannock,* introduced and annotated by Frederick Oughton. London: Neville Spearman, 1966. Oughton's explanations and background material superbly supplement a fascinating diary by the British ace. One receives a feeling that Mannock was at the same time intrigued and repulsed by the war and killing.

Quentin Reynolds, *They Fought For the Sky*. New York: Rinehart, 1957. Distinguished military writer and correspondent Reynolds delivers a readable account of the air war in World War I. He includes biographical material on most aces.

Manfred von Richthofen, *The Red Air Fighter*. London: Greenhill Books, 1999. First published in 1917, the Red Baron's own account of his military service makes fascinating reading. He provides a superb glimpse into aviation in the war and into his mental approach to battle. His writing, although somewhat awkward in places, appeals to the younger reader as well as the adult market.

Edward V. Rickenbacker, *Rickenbacker*. Englewood Cliffs, NJ: Prentice-Hall, 1967. The famed American ace contributes one of the best military memoirs in this volume. Readers will enjoy his thorough account of fighting in World War I, as well as his comments on his postwar career.

Bruce Robertson, ed., *Air Aces of the 1914–1918 War*. Los Angeles: Aero Publishers, 1964. This book contains helpful brief biographies of all the major aces in World War I. Facts rather than drama dominate this work, which is more suitable for a professional audience than a middle school–age group.

Internet Source

www.times1190.freeserve.co.uk/albert.htm. The website of the *Sherwood Times* contains numerous profiles of famous individuals from the region. The section on Capt. Albert Ball was especially helpful.

☆ Index ☆

★ Picture Credits ★

★ About the Author ★

John F. Wukovits is a junior high school teacher and writer from Trenton, Michigan, who specializes in history and biography. Besides biographies of Anne Frank, Jim Carrey, Stephen King, and Martin Luther King Jr. for Lucent, he has written biographies of the World War II commander Adm. Clifton Sprague, Barry Sanders, Tim Allen, Jack Nicklaus, Vince Lombardi, and Wyatt Earp. A graduate of the University of Notre Dame, Wukovits is the father of three daughters—Amy, Julie, and Karen.